HAMMOND

DISCOVERING
MAPS

INTRODUCTION

Suppose you are an explorer, setting forth for a place you have never seen. Will your adventure take you across seas, over land, or into space? Will you have to find your way over broad plains or through thick forests? Will there be treacherous rivers of mud or ice along the way? Perhaps you will have to cross deserts in the scorching sun with little or no water. What if ranges of mountains rise in the distance to block your path? Can you find the best way to get over them before the snow falls?

To succeed in your quest and come safely home, you will have to plan and prepare. What supplies should you carry? An old explorer says that one tool will serve you better than any other. No, it is not a weapon. It is advance knowledge of where you are going. Using it wisely, you can see what lies ahead.

It is a book of maps.

A small map you hold in your hand can show you the world at a single glance. Other maps can give you detailed knowledge of places you've never seen. In which direction should you travel to reach your goal?

How many miles must you go? What kind of land will you pass through: Low or high? Flat or steep? Fields or forests? Grasslands or deserts? Where are the best trails or roads? Are there good, safe harbors for ships? What kinds of weather should you prepare for: Hot or cold? Wet or dry? What kinds of foods might you find along the way? Where will you find settlements of people—places where you can get news and buy supplies? Who claims the lands you will be passing through?

Maps can tell you all these things if you learn how to read them. To say so much in so small a space, mapmakers use a kind of code. This book was written to teach you the basic code of maps. Once you can read a map's symbols, you can unlock its secrets. Then you will be ready to do real detective work with maps. First, you'll learn to identify your own place in time and space. Then you'll be ready to venture out to explore your continent—and your universe. With basic map skills to guide you, who knows what hidden marvels maps might help you find?

Alma Graham

Discovering Maps © COPYRIGHT 2008 BY
HAMMOND WORLD ATLAS CORPORATION

CREDITS

p. 9 bottom Jeff Schultz/Alaska Stock Images, p. 9 top David Young-Wolff/PhotoEdit Inc., p. 9 top David Young-Wolff/PhotoEdit Inc., p. 10 1 Library of Congress, Geography and Map Division, p. 10 2 Northwind Picture Archives, p. 10 3 Library of Congress, Geography and Map Division, p. 10 4 Northwind Picture Archives/Alamy, p. 10 5 Library of Congress Prints and Photographs Division, p. 10 bottom TerraServer, p. 12 bottom Jupiterimages Corporation, p. 14 bottom Ashley Jouhar/Jupiter Images, p. 14 top Dmitriy Rytikov/iStockphoto.com, p. 33 right Visions of America, LLC/Alamy, p. 34 1 Phil Giouvanos, p. 40 bottom Jupiterimages Corporation, p. 40 top FLAG, p. 41 bottom Lise Gagne/iStockphoto.com, p. 54 bottom Jupiterimages Corporation, p. 54 top Forest Woodward/iStockphoto.com, p. 55 bottom franck camhi/iStockphoto.com, p. 58 bottom Jupiterimages Corporation, p. 58 top Jupiterimages Corporation, p. 59 bottom Steven Allan/iStockphoto.com, p. 62 bottom Jaap Hart/iStockphoto.com, p. 62 top Vitalina Rybakova/iStockphoto.com, p. 63 bottom christine balderas/iStockphoto.com, p. 66 bottom Chen How Sia/iStockphoto.com, p. 66 top Frank van den Bergh/iStockphoto.com, p. 67 bottom CPW/iStockphoto.com, p. 70 bottom fotoVoyager/iStockphoto.com, p. 70 top Jupiterimages Corporation, p. 71 bottom Jupiterimages Corporation, p. 74 bottom Steven Profaizer/National Science Foundation, p. 74 top Jan Will/iStockphoto.com, p. 78 1 Jim Padykula, p. 78 2 Lieberman Fredde/Index Stock/Alamy, p. 78 3 DLILLC/CORBIS, p. 78 4 Kirill Putchenko/iStockphoto.com, p. 78 5 Steven Allan/iStockphoto.com, p. 78 6 John Carnemolla/CORBIS, p. 78 7 Melanie Conner/National Science Foundation, p. 80 1 S. Greg Panosian/iStockphoto.com, p. 80 2 Phil Giouvanos, p. 80 3 James Scully/iStockphoto.com, p. 80 4 Andrew Shlykoff/Alamy, p. 80 5 Mark Pearson/Alamy, p. 80 6 Hideo Kurihara/Alamy, p. 80 7 George Steinmetz/CORBIS, p. 82 1 Jupiterimages Corporation, p. 82 2 Phil Giouvanos, p. 82 3 Jupiterimages Corporation, p. 82 4 Majoros Laszlo/iStockphoto.com, p. 82 5 iStockphoto.com, p. 82 6 Jupiterimages Corporation, p. 82 7 Henry Kaiser/National Science Foundation, p. 84 1 Jupiterimages Corporation, p. 84 2 Phil Giouvanos, p. 84 3 Jupiterimages Corporation, p. 84 4 Jupiterimages Corporation, p. 84 5 Jupiterimages Corporation, p. 84 6 Ashley Whitworth/iStockphoto.com, p. 84 7 Jupiterimages Corporation, p. 86 1 Jupiterimages Corporation, p. 86 2 Elena Korenbaum/iStockphoto.com, p. 86 3 blickwinkel/Alamy, p. 86 4 Jupiterimages Corporation, p. 86 5 George Clerk/iStockphoto.com, p. 86 6 Michal Herman/iStockphoto.com, p. 86 7 Alexander Hafemann/iStockphoto.com

CONTENTS

4 Earth's Land and Water

7 Facts About Our Earth

10 How Maps Show Places on Earth

14 Telling Directions on Maps

16 Measuring Distances on Maps

19 Finding Locations on Maps

20 Latitude and Longitude

23 Time Zones

24 Political Maps

26 Landforms and Bodies of Water

28 Physical Maps

30 Distribution Maps

32 Road Maps

34 Navigation by Satellite

36 The World - Physical

38 The World - Political

40 North America: Our Continent

54 South America: Our Southern Neighbor

58 Africa: The Hottest Continent

62 Europe: The Most Crowded Continent

66 Asia: The Largest Continent

70 Australia: The Smallest Continent

74 Antarctica: The Coldest Continent

75 Continent Comparisons

76 Geographic Comparisons

78 Where in the World

88 Map Index

YOUR PLACE **ON EARTH**

Your Earth

You live on the planet Earth. The picture to the right shows the Earth from outer space. From so far away, you can see that the Earth is round. You can even see it has **land** and **water**.

✳ How can you tell the land and water apart?
✳ Why does the Earth look small in the picture?

land

Like Earth, a **globe** is round. The globe below is a model of Earth. It looks like Earth but smaller. On a globe, it is easy to tell land from water. You can clearly see shapes of the land. You can also see the names people have given to places on Earth.

water

THINK ABOUT IT

1. A toy train is a model of a railroad train. A doll or action figure is a model of a person. What other models can you name?

2. How is the globe like the picture of the Earth? How is it different?

Your Half of Earth

The Earth is round. It is shaped like a ball. Something ball-shaped can be called a globe or sphere. Half a sphere is a **hemisphere**. *Hemi* means "half" in Greek. So a hemisphere is our name for half of the Earth.

We can divide the Earth into a northern half and a southern half. You live in the northern half of the Earth. So you live in the **Northern Hemisphere**. Or, we can divide the Earth into an eastern half and a western half. You live in the western half of the Earth. So you live in the **Western Hemisphere**.

Earth's Land and Water

The Earth has seven large areas of land called **continents**. Asia, Africa, North America, South America, Antarctica, Europe and Australia are continents. They are listed here in order of size.

Smaller areas of land with water all around them are called **islands**. Islands are the tops of under water mountains. The smallest continent, Australia, is more than three times bigger than the largest island, Greenland.

The Earth also has five large bodies of water called **oceans**. Find the names of the oceans on the spheres at right. The five oceans are really part of one huge body of water. In fact, you live in a very watery world. Look at the Earth's oceans on a globe. Does the planet Earth have more dry land or more water?

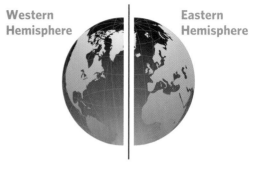

Western Hemisphere
Eastern Hemisphere

Northern Hemisphere

Southern Hemisphere

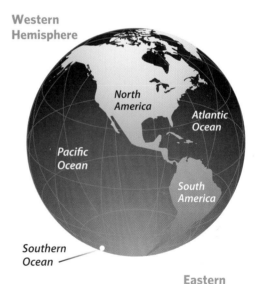

Western Hemisphere

North America
Atlantic Ocean
Pacific Ocean
South America
Southern Ocean

Eastern Hemisphere

Arctic Ocean
Atlantic Ocean
Europe
Asia
Africa
Pacific Ocean
Indian Ocean

THINK ABOUT IT

Look at a globe that you can turn. How much of the Earth can you see at one time? Why?

Your Continent

The sphere at the right shows your continent. It is **North America**. Three of Earth's oceans touch North America. They are the Atlantic Ocean, the Pacific Ocean and the Arctic Ocean.

✸ Which Oceans do not touch North America? (To find out, look at the spheres on page 5.)

There are ten countries on the continent of North America. A **country** has its own land, people and government. It is also called a **nation**. Your country is called the **United States of America**.

✸ Find the United States on the globe.

✸ Find two other large nations of North America.

WESTERN HEMISPHERE

Your Country

The United States is made up of 50 parts called **states**. Of these states, 48 touch one another. Two states, Alaska and Hawaii, are separate. Puerto Rico is not a state but is a part of the United States.

Each state has many towns and cities. Each town and city has neighborhoods and schools.

✸ Start with your school. Tell where you are on Earth. Where you are is your **location**.

THINK ABOUT IT

1. Suppose you live in the United States of America. But suppose you do not live on the continent of North America. Where do you live?

2. In what ways does your location change during the day? In what ways does it stay the same?

FACTS ABOUT **OUR EARTH**

Earth Rotates and Gives Us Days

The Earth is a **planet**. A planet is a large solid body that moves around a star. Our star is the sun. Our planet's movements in space help us measure time.

The Earth's **axis** is an imaginary line that runs through the center of the Earth. The ends of the axis are the **North Pole** and **South Pole**. The Earth turns around its axis the way a top spins. To move this way is to **rotate**. We call the Earth's movement around its axis **rotation**.

It takes 24 hours for the Earth to rotate around its axis. That is why a **day** on Earth is 24 hours long. We have daytime when our part of the Earth faces the sun. We have nighttime when our part of the Earth faces away from the sun. Daytime and nighttime together make a 24-hour day.

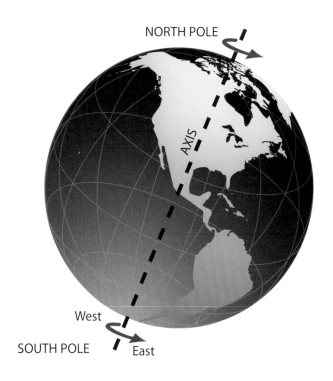

1 ROTATION = 24 HOURS = 1 DAY

Earth's Rotation Gives Us Directions

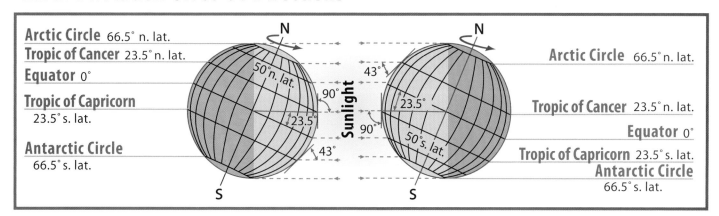

The Earth's rotation also helps us tell **directions**. The four main directions on Earth are **north, south, east** and **west**. North and south are defined by the Earth's axis. To go north means to go toward the North Pole. To go south means to go toward the South Pole. East and west are defined by the Earth's rotation around its axis. The Earth rotates from west to east. That is why the sun seems to rise in the east in the morning. That is why the sun seems to set in the west at night.

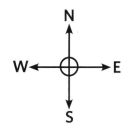

THINK ABOUT IT

On two days a year, the hours of daytime and nighttime are equal. How many hours of daytime do we have then?

7

Earth Revolves and Gives Us Years

The Earth also travels, or **revolves**, around the sun. The path the Earth takes is called an **orbit**. It takes 365 1/4 days for the Earth to make one **revolution**, or trip, around the sun. That is why a **year** on the Earth is 365 days long.

THINK ABOUT IT

Every four years, we usually have a leap year of 366 days. Why?

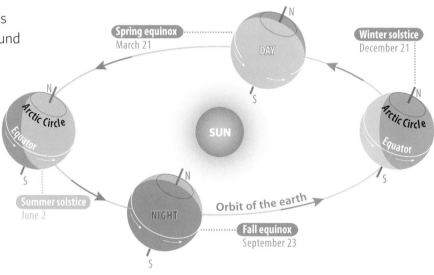

Orbit of the earth

Earth's Positions Gives Us Seasons

Why do seasons change on Earth? This happens because the Earth revolves around the sun. It also happens because the Earth's axis leans to one side. The axis is slanted, or tilted.

In June, the North Pole leans toward the sun. So the northern half of the Earth gets more of the sun's light and heat. Because of this, the weather gets warmer. Summer comes to the Northern Hemisphere. The day that spring becomes summer is the day of longest light.

In December, the North Pole leans away from the sun. So the northern half of the Earth gets less of the sun's light and heat. As a result, the weather gets colder. Winter comes to the Northern Hemisphere. As winter approaches, it gets dark earlier in the evening. The day that fall becomes winter is the day of shortest light.

In the Southern Hemisphere, seasons are just the opposite. The South Pole is tilted toward the sun in December. It is tilted away from the sun in June.

✴ The continent of Australia is in the Southern Hemisphere. When it is summer in Australia what season is it here?

THINK ABOUT IT

1. In June, the North Pole leans toward the sun. This is a cause. Name one or more effects.
2. The Northern Hemisphere has winter. This is an effect. What is the cause?

EDGE OF SUN

VENUS EARTH

MERCURY MARS

MERCURY

JUPITER

SATURN

URANUS

NEPTUNE

PLUTO
(not a planet)

Your Place in Time and Space

You live on the third planet from the sun. You live between the middle of the Earth and the North Pole. You know your continent is North America and your country is the United States. You know what day and month and year it is today. You know how many revolutions the Earth has made since you were born. As you learn about the Earth, you are finding your own special place in time and space.

It's Not Easy Being Pluto

Pluto was once an official planet, but in 2006 it was downgraded to a dwarf planet. The new rules now say that an "offical" planet must do three things:

1) it must orbit the sun,

2) it must be large enough for gravity to have shaped it into a sphere, and

3) it must have cleared other objects out of its orbit.

Because Pluto orbits with many other icy objects, it does not meet the third rule.

LAND OF THE MIDNIGHT SUN

Near the North Pole, the seasons are much different. Because of the tilt of the Earth's axis, the sun is never directly overhead. This means the weather is always cold. Winter at the North Pole is a time of darkness, day and night. The sun never rises.

Summer at the North Pole is a time when the sun never sets. You can see the sun even at midnight. That is why the area near the North Pole is called the "land of the midnight sun."

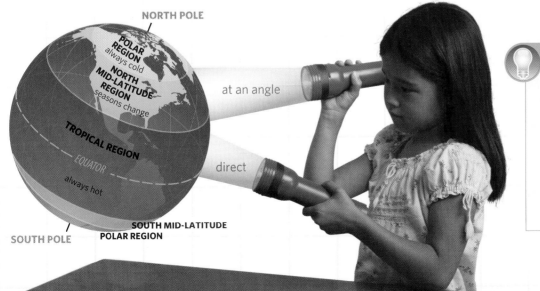

NORTH POLE

POLAR REGION
always cold

NORTH MID-LATITUDE REGION
seasons change

TROPICAL REGION

EQUATOR
always hot

SOUTH MID-LATITUDE
POLAR REGION

SOUTH POLE

at an angle

direct

THINK ABOUT IT

1. Look at the sphere to the left. Do you live in a part of the Earth where seasons change?

2. How many revolutions has the Earth made since you were born?

HOW MAPS SHOW **PLACES ON EARTH**

A **map** is a flat drawing of a place or places on the Earth. A map can show the whole Earth, as a globe does. Or, a map can show any part of the Earth.

A map shows a place from above. It is like a picture taken from high in the air or from outer space. Such a picture is called an **aerial photograph**.

The aerial photograph above shows part of Washington, D.C. This is a view from an airplane. The map opposite it on page 11 is a drawing of the same area.

page 11

PAST AND PRESENT

Today, aerial photographs help mapmakers make better maps. In the past, people could not take photographs of Earth from the air. They had to explore a place before they could map it.

An explorer had to sail along a coast to draw a map of the coastline. Explorers had to cross our continent in canoes, on horseback, and on foot. Only then could they draw maps showing what North America was like. They found forests and deserts, lakes and rivers and plains and mountains. They also discovered the best trails to follow. All these features can be shown on maps.

MAPPING AMERICA
Then and Now

1500s	1600s	1700s	1800s	1900s
1507 First Map showing "America" as a "continent"	**1612** Map of Virginia by John Smith	**1755** Colonist Lewis Evans maps the "Middle British Colonies in America"	**1804-1806** Lewis and Clark explore and map western North America **1826** First photograph made	**1903** First successful airplane flight **1957** First artificial earth satellite launched **1972** First Landsat satellite photographs Earth

WASHINGTON, D.C.

An aerial view of Washington, D.C.

Reading Symbols on Maps

A map has to show a large area in a small space. That is why mapmakers use symbols. A map **symbol** is a drawing or color that stands for a real place or thing. A special section on each map shows what the symbols mean. This section is called the map **key**, or **legend**.

The map below shows Washington, D.C. Look at the map symbols in the key. Find the symbol for buildings. It has a special color. Now find the U.S. Capitol on the map. Then compare that map symbol with the actual Capitol in the aerial photograph on page 10.

The secrets of each map are locked inside its symbols. Some special symbols appear on many maps. You will find them when you use a book of maps, called an **atlas**.

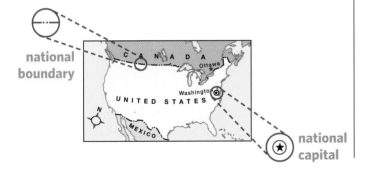

Map symbols may be simple **shapes**, such as a dot or star. On most maps of a large area, a black dot ● stands for a city. Many mapmakers use a star ★ to stand for a state capital. Others show a state capital as a dot in a circle ⊙. A star in a circle ⊛ usually marks the capital of a country, or a national capital. Washington, D.C., is the capital of the United States. Find it on the map of the United States at the bottom of page 17.

Lines are also used as symbols on maps. A line may mark a road or river. Or it maybe a **border**, also called a **boundary**. A boundary is a line that separates one city, state or nation from another. Boundaries may be marked by solid lines ——— or broken lines —·—·— of dots and dashes.

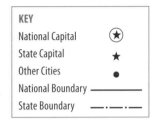

KEY

National Capital	⊛
State Capital	★
Other Cities	●
National Boundary	———
State Boundary	—·—·—

THINK ABOUT IT

1. In what ways are the map and the photograph alike? In what ways do they differ?

2. What information does the map give you that the photograph does not? Name as many examples as you can.

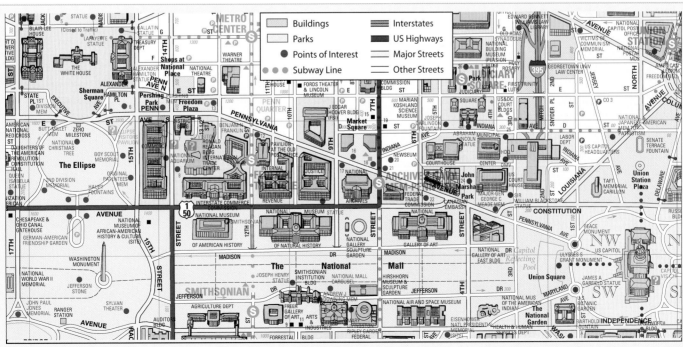

A map of Washington, D.C.

Other symbols are more than lines or shapes. They may be **drawings** that suggest the thing they stand for. Symbols showing natural resources are of this type. A drawing of an oil derrick may show where oil wells are found. Crossed pickaxes may stand for metals that people dig out of the ground.

💡 THINK ABOUT IT

Test your powers of **inference**. You may recognize more symbols than you think. Match each map symbol at the left with the thing it stands for on the right.

SYMBOL		NAME
1.	⟩	a. railroad
2.	▲	b. airport
3.	⬆	c. river
4.	✈	d. park
5.	+++++++	e. mountain

LEADING PRODUCTS OF NORTH AMERICA

⏰ PAST AND PRESENT

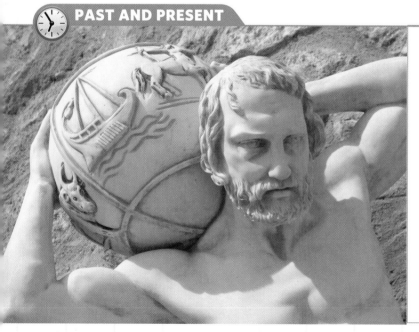

In Greek myths of long ago, Atlas was a giant. He was huge and was very strong and powerful. In fact, it was his job to hold up the sky on his shoulders!

Mapmakers four centuries ago knew the old story of Atlas. They put drawings of him in their books of maps. His picture was right on the title page, holding up a globe of the Earth. Because of this, many people today think Atlas held up the whole world—not just the sky. Either way, it must have been a very heavy load!

To this day, a map book is called an atlas. An atlas shows places on Earth. Sometimes an atlas also has a map of the skies.

Maps are easier to read when **colors** are used. Colors are really another kind of symbol. They can tell you many things.

Colors help us tell land from water easily. Usually water is shown by the color blue. Because of this, blue is rarely used to show any other feature. Land can be shown by any other colors.

Colors can also help you tell one state or nation from another. On the map at the right, notice how different colors separate the United States from Canada. Alaska is the same color as the United States. This tells you that Alaska is part of the United States, not part of Canada.

Mapmakers use bright colors to show important information.

✳ Look at the road map on Page 31. What types of things are shown in red? Is it easier to see some roads because they are red?

Sometimes map colors show whether land is low and flat, or high and full of mountains. Notice how colors are used on the Alaska map below. The brown colors show mountains. Green shows us where the low, flat land is located. Does Alaska have more mountains or lowlands?

Map colors can also show whether lands are hot or cold, rainy or dry, empty or full of people.

✳ Make your own map. What would you use different colors to show?

NORTH AMERICA

Arctic Ocean

Greenland (Denmark)

Alaska (U.S.)

ATLANTIC OCEAN

CANADA

PACIFIC OCEAN

UNITED STATES

MEXICO

Gulf of Mexico

Puerto Rico (U.S.)

Central America

THINK ABOUT IT

What colors would you use to show these kinds of places on a map?

1. cold places
2. warm or hot places
3. dry places
4. mountains

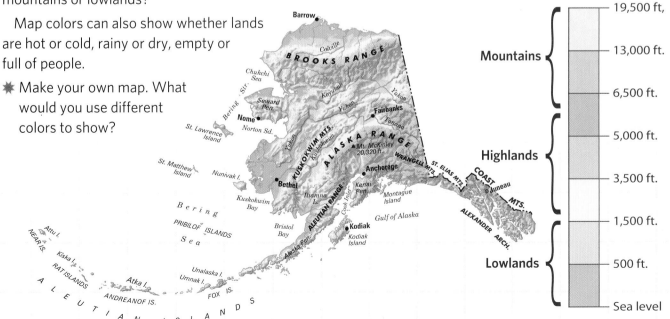

Barrow

Colville

BROOKS RANGE

Chukchi Sea

Bering Str.

Seward Pen.

Koyukuk

Yukon

Nome

St. Lawrence Island

Norton Sd.

Yukon

Fairbanks

Tanana

St. Matthew Island

Nunivak I.

KUSKOKWIM MTS.

Kuskokwim

ALASKA RANGE

Mt. McKinley 20,320 ft.

WRANGELL MTS.

ST. ELIAS MTS.

COAST

Bethel

Iliamna L.

Kenai Pen.

Anchorage

Juneau

Kuskokwim Bay

ALEUTIAN RANGE

Cook Inlet

Montague Island

MTS.

Bering

PRIBILOF ISLANDS

Bristol Bay

Gulf of Alaska

ALEXANDER ARCH.

Sea

Kodiak

Attu I.

NEAR IS.

Kiska I.

RAT ISLANDS

Atka I.

ANDREANOF IS.

Umnak I.

Unalaska I.

FOX IS.

ALEUTIAN ISLANDS

Alaska Pen.

Kodiak Island

Mountains	19,500 ft.
	13,000 ft.
	6,500 ft.
Highlands	5,000 ft.
	3,500 ft.
Lowlands	1,500 ft.
	500 ft.
	Sea level

TELLING DIRECTIONS ON MAPS

Maps have symbols other than those shown in the map key. Every map needs at least one symbol to show direction. A real **compass** is a small magnet. It has a movable needle that always points north. The most common symbol for direction is a straight arrow pointing north. It is called a **direction arrow**.

compass   compass rose

In the past, mapmakers often drew fancy direction arrows. Some of these pointers looked like petals on a rose. So a direction symbol with many pointers came to be called a **compass rose**.

A compass rose is a drawing used on a map. It has an arrow or pointer to show where north is. Often it shows all four **cardinal directions**. These are the four main directions on the Earth: north, south, east and west.

NORTH AMERICA

Mapmakers abbreviate the cardinal directions. They use the first letter of each word. N stands for north, S for south, E for east and W for west.

When you know where north is, you can find the other directions. South is opposite north. East is right of north. West is left of north.

There are also **intermediate** ("in-between") **directions**. They help you to be more exact in telling where things are located. **Northeast** (NE) is between north and east. **Southwest** (SW) is between south and west. Where is **southeast**? Where is **northwest**?

Some maps show cardinal and intermediate directions on a compass rose. Now you know what this map symbol means.

Mapmakers usually draw maps so that north is at the top of the page. This is not always true, though. Remember: north and south are not the same as up and down. Up means "toward the sky." North means "toward the North Pole."

UNITED STATES

WASHINGTON
OREGON
IDAHO
MONTANA
NORTH DAKOTA
SOUTH DAKOTA
WYOMING
MINNESOTA
WISCONSIN
MICHIGAN
NEW HAMPSHIRE
VERMONT
MAINE
NEW YORK
MASSACHUSETTS
RHODE ISLAND
CONNECTICUT
NEW JERSEY
DELAWARE
MARYLAND
NEVADA
UTAH
COLORADO
NEBRASKA
IOWA
ILLINOIS
INDIANA
OHIO
PENNSYLVANIA
WEST VIRGINIA
VIRGINIA
CALIFORNIA
ARIZONA
NEW MEXICO
KANSAS
OKLAHOMA
MISSOURI
KENTUCKY
TENNESSE
NORTH CAROLINA
SOUTH CAROLINA
ARKANSAS
MISSISSIPPI
ALABAMA
GEORGIA
TEXAS
LOUISIANA
FLORIDA

𝒩

North and south refer to fixed points on the planet Earth. You cannot go farther south than the South Pole. However, there are no natural stopping points for east and west. You could travel all the way around the Earth by traveling east. If you did this, where would you end up? We use map directions in two major ways. We may use them to describe **absolute** (unchanging) **locations**. For example, in the United States, Georgia is in the South. New Jersey is in the East. Arizona is in the Southwest. Oregon is in the Northwest.

We may also use directions to tell **relative** (changing) **locations**. Find Illinois on the map above. If you are in Wisconsin, Illinois is south of you. If you are in Pennsylvania, Illinois is west of you. Illinois is not moving. You are changing your point of view.

Now try using the intermediate directions. To get from Florida to Illinois, you go northwest. To get from Montana to Illinois, which way do you go?

✳ Play a game. Give hints and let someone guess where you are. For example: "To get to Pennsylvania, I go north. To get to Virginia, I go south. To get to West Virginia, I go west. To get to Delaware, I go east. Where am I?"

💡 **THINK ABOUT IT**

1. Imagine you are in a small round room with windows on all sides. Every window faces south. You see a bear outside. Where are you? What color is the bear?

2. What are the abbreviations for southeast and northwest?

3. Let's go for a trip. Use your sense of direction: northeast, northwest, southeast, or southwest? In what direction do we head?

   a. From New Jersey to Maine, go _____.

   b. From Michigan to New Mexico, go _____.

   c. From Georgia to Idaho, go _____.

   d. From Wyoming to Louisiana, go _____.

MEASURING DISTANCES ON MAPS

Maps not only show you where places are located. They can help you figure out how far one place is from another. When you measure "how far," you are measuring **distance**.

The distance between places on Earth is measured in miles or kilometers. On a map, though, two big cities may be only an inch apart. When you measure distance on a map, you need to change it into real distance on Earth. To do this, you use a distance scale.

A **distance scale** is a horizontal line or bar on a map. Look at the scale above. One bar shows what the map distance equals in miles. The other shows what the map distance equals in kilometers. The mapmaker lets a small length stand for a larger one. On the map, how far is Atlanta from Miami in inches? How many miles does this stand for?

THINK ABOUT IT

1. Look at the map above. What is the map distance from Minneapolis to Pittsburgh?

2. Can you drive from Minneapolis to Pittsburgh in a straight line? Why or why not?

3. Suppose you went from Portland, Oregon to Atlanta, Georgia by bus. Would the road distance be the same as the map distance? Or would the road distance be longer or shorter? Why?

PAST AND PRESENT

In the United States, we use two different systems of measurement. One is called the **customary system**. It measures distances in inches, feet, yards and miles. In olden times, people used parts of their body as standards for measuring. An **inch** was the width of a man's thumb. A **foot** was the length of his foot. A man held out his arm to measure a **yard**. It was the distance from his nose to the tip of his middle finger.

Since people were different sizes, they had to agree on standard measurements. The result was our customary system. In it, 12 inches equal a foot, and 3 feet equal a yard. A **mile** is 5,280 feet.

The more modern system of measurement is the **metric system**. It measures distances in centimeters, meters and kilometers. These are standard sizes based on counting by 10's. One **centimeter** equals 1/100 meter, or 2/5 inch. One **kilometer** equals 1000 meters, or 3/5 mile. Metric measurements are now used around the world.

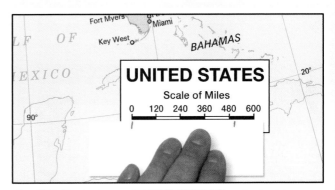

The two pictures above show you how to measure the distance between two cities on a map. The cities in the picture on the left are state capitals: Topeka, Kansas, and Indianapolis, Indiana.

First, locate the two city dots. Then, mark off the space between them on the edge of a piece of paper. Next, place your paper under the scale of miles on the map. Put the first mark at zero. The second mark falls one quarter of the way to the right of 480. The distance between these cities is about 510 miles.

Next, measure the distance between Topeka, Kansas and Cleveland, Ohio. This time, your marked section is longer than the distance scale. Put your first mark at zero. Add a mark where the scale ends. Label this new mark 600. Then move the 600 mark to zero and start over. What new distance do you get? Add the new distance to 600. What is the total distance in miles? Now practice measuring distance using the map and Scale of Miles at the top of page 16. How far is it from New York to Boston? From Dallas to New Orleans? From Chicago to Atlanta?

Map Scale

A **scale** is a means of measuring something. You stand on a scale to measure your weight. Scale also means the size of one thing compared to another. Map scale lets you compare sizes on a map to sizes on Earth.

The same place can be shown on maps of different sizes. Look at the maps below. The first map shows only the state of California. The second shows California as part of our nation, the United States. The third map shows California's place on the continent of North America. As the area shown on the map gets larger, the map scale gets smaller. California seems to be getting smaller, too. Actually, its real size on Earth remains the same.

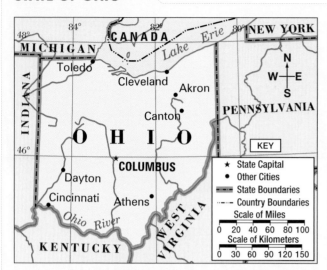

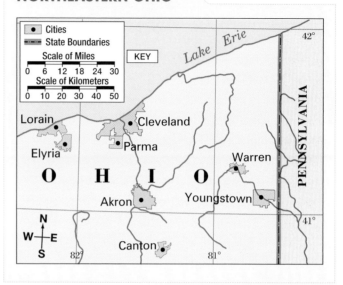

Look at the maps of Ohio above. One map shows the whole state. The other shows five cities in the northeastern part of the state. One inch on the map of five cities equals 32 miles. One inch on the state map equals 85 miles.

Measure the map distance between Cleveland and Canton on the state map above. Use the distance scale. How many miles does this tell you it is? Now, measure the map distance on the five cities map. Use the scale on that map to find out how far it is. What are your answers? Should these answers be the same?

Usually a map of a large area, such as a state or entire nation, must be drawn on a small scale. Not much detail can be shown. For example, on a map of a state, cities may appear as just dots. Rivers may be just a thin line.

A map of a smaller area can be drawn on a larger scale in the same space. More detail can be added. For example, a map of a city or neighborhood may include streets, highways, parks and even important buildings. Rivers may be shown by drawing both banks, and may even include symbols for docks and bridges.

Mapmakers decide what information their maps need to show. Then they choose the best scale to suit the purpose.

The map of the largest area–the state–is drawn to a smaller scale. That means that places on the map

look smaller. The cities seem closer together. Still, the real distance between the cities has not changed.

You can be a mapmaker too.

✳ Plan a map of your room. What scale might you use?

✳ Measure your room. Using these measurements, how large would your map be if one inch equals one foot?

✳ How large would your map be if one inch equals two feet?

THINK ABOUT IT

Have you mastered distance measurement? Turn to the map of the United States on page 43. Measure the distances between the following state capitals. Use the scale of miles to change the map distance into real distance on the Earth.

1. Sacramento, California to Carson City, Nevada

2. Denver, Colorado to Santa Fe, New Mexico

3. Des Moines, Iowa to Pierre, South Dakota

4. Atlanta, Georgia to Columbia, South Carolina

5. Albany, New York to Augusta, Maine

FINDING LOCATIONS ON MAPS

Have you ever given directions in a neighborhood? You often refer to crossing streets, or **intersections**. Mapmakers can create intersections for you on maps by using crossing lines. To see how this works, look at the map of Pennsylvania below. The mapmaker has drawn lines from top to bottom and from side to side. These crossing lines divide the map into a pattern of squares called a **grid**.

Now look around all four sides of the map. The letters A, B, C and D go across the top and bottom. The numbers 1, 2 and 3 go down both sides. Thus, each square in the grid has both a letter and a number. The letter and the number are the address of the square.

Find square C-3. First, at the top of the map, find the letter C. Then, at the side of the map, find the number 3. Move one finger down column C. Move another finger across row 3. Your fingers will meet at square C-3. The capital of Pennsylvania is there. What is it?

Now find square A-1. It includes Pennsylvania's northwestern boundary. What city is in square A-1? Now find square A-2. It is in western Pennsylvania. What city is in square A-2? Pennsylvania's largest city is in square D-3. What is it?

Have you ever tried to locate a place by looking in an atlas? A **map index** makes places easy to find. A map index is an alphabetical listing of place names on a map or maps. For each place name in the atlas, it gives a page number and a grid square.

PENNSYLVANIA AND NEIGHBORING STATES

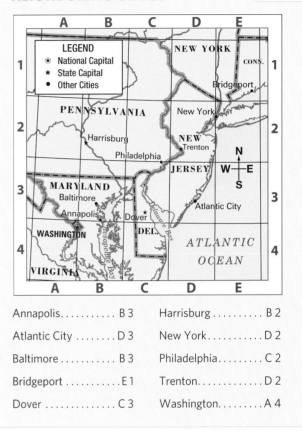

Annapolis...........B 3	Harrisburg...........B 2
Atlantic City........D 3	New York...........D 2
Baltimore...........B 3	Philadelphia.........C 2
Bridgeport..........E 1	Trenton.............D 2
Dover..............C 3	Washington.........A 4

✳ Look at the map of Pennsylvania and neighboring states above. Suppose you are in Dover, Delaware. You want to find Bridgeport, Connecticut. Use the index below the map. In what square is Dover? Find it on the map. In what square is Bridgeport? To get from Dover to Bridgeport, which way would you go?

STATE OF PENNSYLVANIA

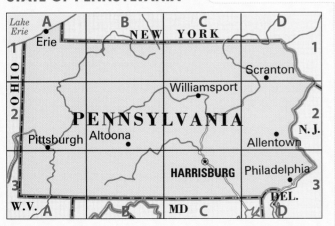

THINK ABOUT IT

How many state capitals are shown on the map above? List each state capital and its grid location.

CAPITAL	GRID LOCATION
_____	_____
_____	_____
_____	_____
_____	_____

LATITUDE AND LONGITUDE

To find a place exactly, you need crossing lines that create an intersection. This is a grid system. One grid system is used by mapmakers all over the world. It helps you locate any place on Earth. It is known as the latitude and longitude grid.

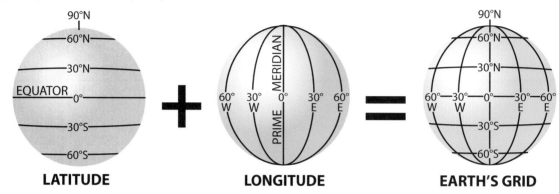

LATITUDE + LONGITUDE = EARTH'S GRID

Latitude

Halfway between the North Pole and the South Pole is an imaginary line, the **equator**. The equator goes around the middle of the Earth like a belt. It divides our planet into the Northern Hemisphere and the Southern Hemisphere.

The equator is a line of **latitude**. The other lines of latitude are north and south of the equator. They are parallel to the equator. Parallel lines run in the same direction and are an equal distance apart at all points. They never meet. Thus, lines of latitude are also called **parallels**. They run east-west around the globe.

Parallels measure distance north or south of the equator. This distance is measured in **degrees**. Earth, as a circle, is divided into 360 degrees (360°).

We measure latitude starting at the equator. Its address is zero degrees latitude, or 0° latitude. The distance from the equator to the North Pole is 1/4 of the distance around the Earth. So the North Pole is at 90 degrees north latitude. The distance from the equator to the South Pole is also 1/4 of the distance around the Earth. What is the latitude of the South Pole?

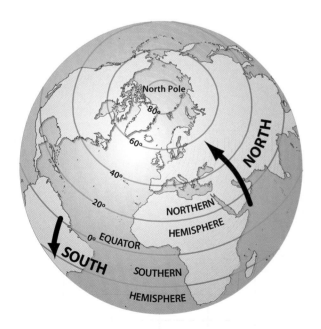

You can measure your latitude by using the night sky. In the Northern Hemisphere, find the North Star, Polaris. Extend one arm toward the star. Extend your other arm toward the horizon. The **horizon** is the point where the sky and land seem to meet in the distance.

Use a protractor to measure the number of degrees between your outstretched arms. If the angle is 40 degrees, you are located at 40° north. At the equator, Polaris appears right at the horizon. You are at 0° latitude.

✳ What latitude do you find if you try this?

✳ How close is this to an accurate figure found in an atlas?

Longitude

Another set of imaginary lines helps us to measure distance east and west. These are lines of **longitude**. Each line of longitude runs from the North Pole to the South Pole. These lines are also called **meridians**.

Each meridian travels halfway around the Earth. Along its imaginary journey it crosses each line of latitude once. These intersections mark an exact location for any point on Earth.

Longitude lines are measured in degrees, just as latitude. However, there is no natural starting or stopping point for east and west. So mapmakers need a place to begin. They call that line of longitude the **prime meridian**. Its address is zero degrees longitude, or 0° longitude.

From the prime meridian, you can travel west halfway around the Earth to the 180° west longitude line. You may also travel east halfway around the Earth to the 180° east longitude line. At the 180° line, east meets west: 180° E and 180° W are the same line!

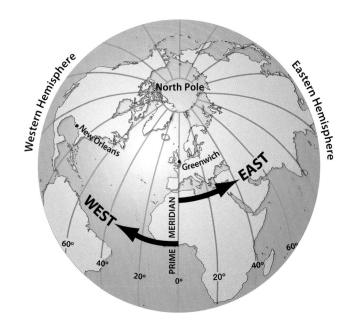

Look at the sphere above. Notice that lines of longitude do not stay the same distance from each other. Meridians are farthest apart at the equator. They are closer together at the poles.

In fact, one degree east-west is 69 miles at the equator. At the poles there is no distance between each degree line. They all meet at the same spot!

PAST AND PRESENT

Today, the prime meridian passes through Greenwich, England, part of the city of London. But it wasn't always so.

Until the 19th century, mapmakers would place the zero degree line wherever they wished. Often it was shown running through the capital city of the nation where they lived. Paris was the location of the prime meridian for French mapmakers. Rome was at zero degrees longitude for Italian mapmakers.

In 1884, 25 nations finally agreed on the **Greenwich Meridian**. In time, mapmakers of other countries also began using that line as zero degrees longitude.

However, if the Greenwich Meridian is used to divide Earth into Eastern and Western Hemispheres, the continents of Europe and Africa are partly in both hemispheres. For this reason, even now, some mapmakers would like to move the location of the prime meridian.

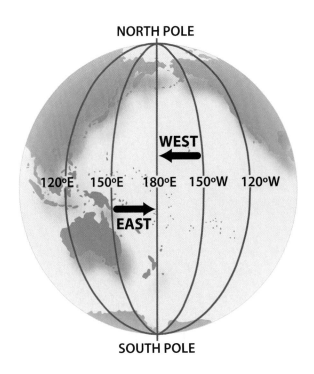

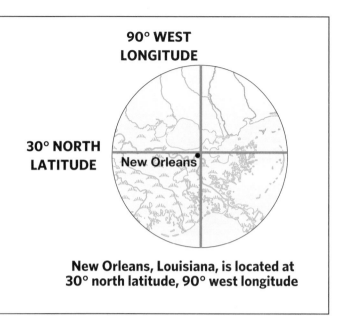

90° WEST LONGITUDE

30° NORTH LATITUDE

New Orleans

New Orleans, Louisiana, is located at 30° north latitude, 90° west longitude

SEVEN EASTERN STATES

LEGEND
⊛ National Capital
★ State Capital
• Other Cities

NEW YORK
CONN.
Bridgeport
New York
PENNSYLVANIA
Harrisburg
NEW
Trenton
Philadelphia
JERSEY
MARYLAND
Baltimore
Atlantic City
Annapolis
Dover
DEL.
WASHINGTON
ATLANTIC OCEAN
VIRGINIA

You can use parallels and meridians to write addresses for any place on Earth. The map above shows the address of New Orleans, Louisiana. How would you write this address?

Find the global address of Philadelphia, Pennsylvania on the map above on the right. Philadelphia is at 40° north latitude and 75° west longitude. These numbers and directions are the **coordinates** of Philadelphia. So, 40° N, 75° W is the address of the intersection on the Earth at which Philadelphia is found.

To find the coordinates of Trenton, New Jersey on the map above, a longer address is needed. Each degree of latitude and longitude may be divided into sixty **minutes**. The address for Trenton is 40 degrees, 13 minutes north latitude and 74 degrees, 45 minutes west latitude. This is written: 40° 13′ N, 74° 45′ W.

💡 **THINK ABOUT IT**

1. How would you write the address for New Orleans, Louisiana in degrees and minutes?

2. Use the map above. What city is at 39° N, 77° W?

3. If you were standing in New Orleans at night, how many degrees above the horizon would you have to extend your arm to point to the North Star, Polaris?

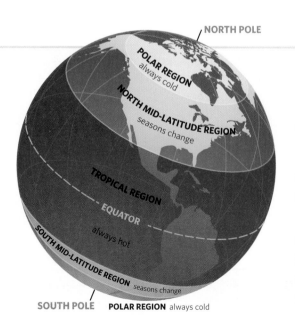

NORTH POLE

POLAR REGION
always cold

NORTH MID-LATITUDE REGION
seasons change

TROPICAL REGION

EQUATOR
always hot

SOUTH MID-LATITUDE REGION
seasons change

SOUTH POLE   POLAR REGION always cold

Latitude Affects Climate

The latitude of a place affects its **climate**, or usual pattern of weather. Areas near the equator remain hot all year. Lands near the North Pole and South Pole are usually cold.

In between the equator and the poles is an area of changing seasons. This area is called the **mid-latitudes**. Here, in the Northern Hemisphere, warm summers arrive in the middle of the year. Colder winters begin as the year ends. In the Southern Hemisphere, these seasons are just the opposite.

TIME ZONES

Because the Earth rotates, some places have daylight while other places have darkness. Wherever you are, it is noon when the sun is at its highest point overhead. However, noon and lunchtime for you may be sunset and suppertime for someone in Europe.

We need to know what time it is all over the world. To do this, we have divided the Earth into **time zones**. It is the same time at any place in the same time zone. Each day is 24 hours long. Each time zone represents one hour. How many time zones does the Earth have?

Longitude Affects Time Zones

Just as latitude affects climate, longitude affects time. In fact, the word meridian means "midday", or "noon." When the sun is directly above a meridian, it is noon there. Our abbreviations **A.M.** and **P.M.** mean "before noon" and "after noon." These words come from the Latin words *Ante Meridian* and *Post Meridian.*

Divide Earth's 360° by the 24 hours in a day. You will get 15°. Each time zone is about 15° of longitude in width.

Earth rotates from west to east. Thus a day starts and ends first in the east. So when you enter a new time zone going west, what happens to the time?

For most of its length, the 180th meridian forms the **International Date Line**. This is an imaginary line marking the spot where a new calendar day starts. On the east longitude side of the line, it is one day later than on the west longitude side. Thus, when you cross this line, you gain or lose a whole day!

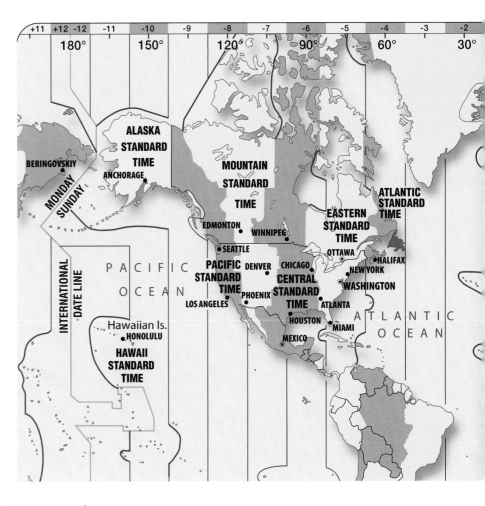

THINK ABOUT IT

Use the time zone map above.

1. You are having supper in New York at 6:00 P.M. For your friend, it is only 1:00 P.M. and lunchtime. In what state does your friend live?

2. You are in Miami, Florida. A friend in Los Angeles, California phones you at 4:00 P.M. Pacific Time. What time is it in Miami when you get the call?

3. It is noon in Seattle, Washington. What time is it in these places?

    a. Phoenix, Arizona

    b. Atlanta, Georgia

    c. Houston, Texas

    d. Anchorage, Alaska

    e. Honolulu, Hawaii

4. When it is 10:00 A.M. Sunday in Honolulu, Hawaii, what time is it in Beringovskiy?

POLITICAL MAPS

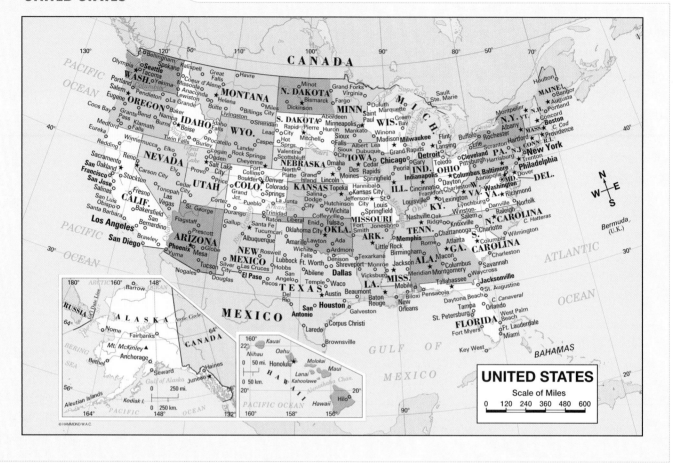

A **political map** shows the lines that divide one nation, state, county or city from another. These are **political boundaries**. People set political boundaries, and people can change them.

The map above is a political map of the United States. The United States is made up of 50 states. Of these, 48 states are **contiguous**, or touch each other. The 49th state, Alaska, touches Canada's northwest border. The 50th state, Hawaii, is near the middle of the Pacific Ocean.

Political Map Insets

On maps of the United States, Alaska and Hawaii are often shown in boxes called **insets**. Both states are too far away from the others to be shown at an accurate distance on the main map. Separating these states in an inset is one way mapmakers let us compare two different places.

✷ Find the Alaska inset on the map above.

Notice that Alaska is drawn to a smaller scale than the main map. Alaska is really the largest state and the one farthest north. You can see its relative size and position on the North America map on page 25.

Insets are often used to show more detail in a crowded area. By drawing the inset at a larger scale, the mapmaker can include more information. Areas around large cities where there are many towns are often shown this way.

THINK ABOUT IT

1. On the map above, is the Hawaii inset drawn at a smaller or larger scale than the main map?

2. Which state is farthest south? How can you tell on the map above?

3. Which state is farthest west?

Political Map Symbols

The key to a political map may show the symbols used for political boundaries and capital cities. The **capital** of a state or nation is the city where the central government is located. The capital of the United States is not in any state. It is in a federal district, the District of Columbia, or D.C.

The map on the right is a political map of North America. On this map, different colors show where one nation stops and another starts. Lines are also drawn on the map to serve as symbols for national boundaries.

✴ Find the capital of Canada on the map of North America. Then, name the national capital located at 20° north latitude, 100° west longitude. Can you give the latitude and longitude location of Washington, D.C.?

✴ Next, find Puerto Rico on the main map. Puerto Rico is not a state. It is a separate part of the United States called a **Commonwealth**. Puerto Ricans are citizens of the United States.

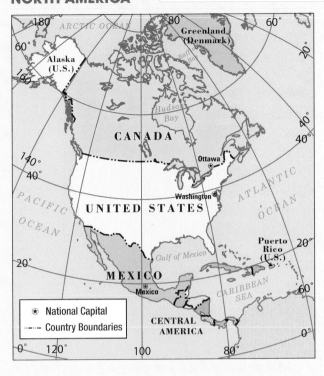

NORTH AMERICA

Key:
✴ National Capital
-·-·- Country Boundaries

More About Political Boundaries

Some political boundaries follow the curving lines of coasts, rivers or mountains. Others are straight lines marked on maps but invisible in the real world. Often, straight boundaries follow lines of latitude or longitude.

You can find examples of these kinds of boundaries on the map to the left. It shows the Southeastern states. Notice the irregular eastern boundaries of the states on the Atlantic coast.

✴ Find the line of 35° north latitude. It forms the entire southern boundary of Tennessee. What three states have this 35th parallel as their northern boundary?

SOUTHEASTERN STATES

Key:
✴ National Capital
★ State Capital · Cities
Scale of Miles
0 60 120 180 240 300
Scale of Kilometers
0 100 200 300 400 500

THINK ABOUT IT

1. If you take a trip from one state to another, would you see the boundary lines as you cross them? What if the boundary line were the same as a river?

2. How might you tell when you leave one state and enter another?

3. How would you tell when you left one country and entered another?

LANDFORMS AND BODIES OF WATER

Unlike political boundaries, some symbols shown on maps are visible on Earth. Our planet has different shapes of land called **landforms**. The highest form of land on Earth is a **mountain**.

A single mountain, or its pointed top, may be called a **peak**. A low place, where it is easier to cross the mountains, is a **pass**. A group of mountains is a **mountain range**. A series of ranges makes up a **mountain system**. The land along the top of connected mountains is a **ridge**.

Some mountains are known as volcanoes. A **volcano** is built up by hot melted rock ejected from an opening in the earth. Many volcanoes are shaped like cones.

In high, cold mountains, glaciers may form. A **glacier** is a huge, slow-moving mass of ice that flows across the land.

Two other kinds of high land are hills and plateaus. A **hill** is not as high as a mountain. A steep-sided hill that is flat on top is called a **mesa**. Hills near the bottom of a mountain are called **foothills**.

A **plateau** is a large area of high land that is flat on top. It is also called a **tableland**. A **piedmont** is a plateau region extending from foothills to a place at which the land drops. This point is called the **fall line**. Here, **waterfalls** form where a river drops to a lower level.

An area of low land between hills or mountains is a **valley**. A valley often has a river running through it. A **canyon** is a narrow valley with high, steep sides. The Grand Canyon in Arizona was carved by the Colorado River flowing over a plateau.

A **plain** is a large area of flat land. There are plains in the middle of North America and along the coasts. A **coast** is land bordering an ocean or sea. Coastal plains are lowlands. Swamps are found near the coast. **Swamps** are lowlands which are mostly covered with shallow water.

Along a coast, you will also find peninsulas, or "almost islands." A **peninsula** is land surrounded by water on all sides but one. An **isthmus** is a

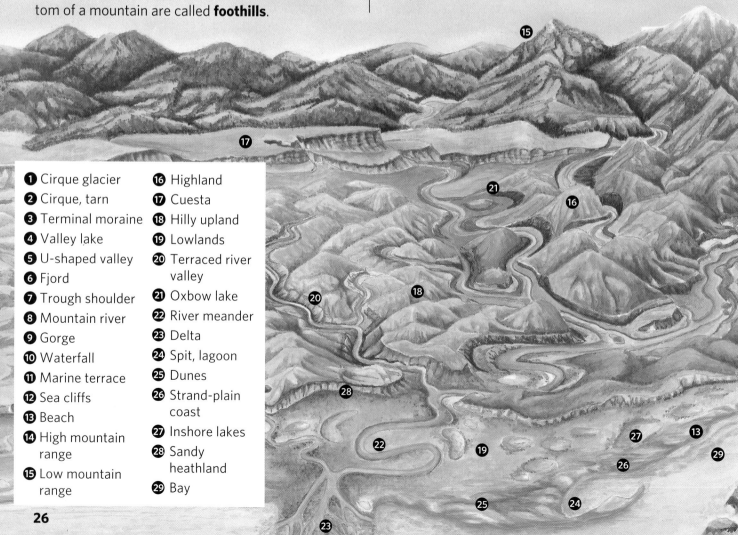

1. Cirque glacier
2. Cirque, tarn
3. Terminal moraine
4. Valley lake
5. U-shaped valley
6. Fjord
7. Trough shoulder
8. Mountain river
9. Gorge
10. Waterfall
11. Marine terrace
12. Sea cliffs
13. Beach
14. High mountain range
15. Low mountain range
16. Highland
17. Cuesta
18. Hilly upland
19. Lowlands
20. Terraced river valley
21. Oxbow lake
22. River meander
23. Delta
24. Spit, lagoon
25. Dunes
26. Strand-plain coast
27. Inshore lakes
28. Sandy heathland
29. Bay

narrow strip of land joining larger land areas. It may join a peninsula to the mainland. A **cape** is a point of land that projects out into an ocean or sea. You know that an **island** is a piece of land completely surrounded by water. A large group of islands is an **archipelago**.

Bodies of water are also shown on maps and in the picture below. A **river** is a large, natural stream that carries water. The **source** of a river, or place where it starts, is usually in the highlands. It may be a **lake**, a body of water completely surrounded by land. It may be a **spring** bubbling up out of the earth. Or it may be melting ice and snow from a glacier.

The **mouth of a river** is the place where it empties into a larger body of water. A river may drop rich soil at its mouth to form a low, triangular plain called a **delta**. A river or stream which flows into

a larger river is a **tributary.** The land drained by a river and its tributaries is its **drainage basin**. A ridge separating drainage basins is a **divide**.

A **sea** is a large body of water smaller than an ocean. A **gulf** or **bay** is usually connected to an ocean or sea and is partly surrounded by land. An **inlet** is a small bay. A long, narrow inlet with high, steep banks is a **fjord**.

A passage of water connecting two larger bodies of water may be called a **strait** or **sound**. Usually a strait is very narrow. A sound often separates an island and the mainland.

THINK ABOUT IT

1. Look at the drawing of landforms and bodies of water. Where would you build:

    a. a road across the mountains?

    b. a seaport city?

    c. a bridge or tunnel?

    d. a railroad from mountains to coast?

2. Where might you find a vacation resort?

PHYSICAL MAPS

sea level

valley

plain

mountain peak

A **physical map** shows Earth's landforms and bodies of water. It is a way of picturing what the land looks like in different places. Earth has **highlands**, such as mountains and plateaus, and **lowlands**, such as plains and valleys. Symbols on a map can show how high or low the land is.

The height of land is its altitude or elevation. To measure the land's **elevation**, you start at sea level, not ground level. **Sea level** is the height of the ocean where it meets the land along the coast.

Suppose you wanted to find the elevation of Cadillac Mountain on Mount Desert Island off the coast of Maine. You would measure straight up from sea level to a point even with the top of the mountain. The elevation of Cadillac Mountain is about 1,500 feet.

Next, suppose you want to measure the elevation of Pikes Peak in Colorado. That mountain is only 7,500 feet above ground level, but over 14,000 feet above sea level. You would need to know how high above sea level the ground at the bottom of the mountain is before you start to measure.

The most common way to show elevation on a physical map is with color. Different colors are used for different elevation ranges, from land below sea level to the highest mountains. Lowlands are usually shown as green. Highlands are usually orange, red or brown.

Look at the stairstep drawing and the physical map below. North America's coastal plains are between sea level and 500 feet in elevation. Inland are higher plains going up to 2,000 feet and up to 5,000 feet. The Great Plains

NORTH AMERICA - PHYSICAL

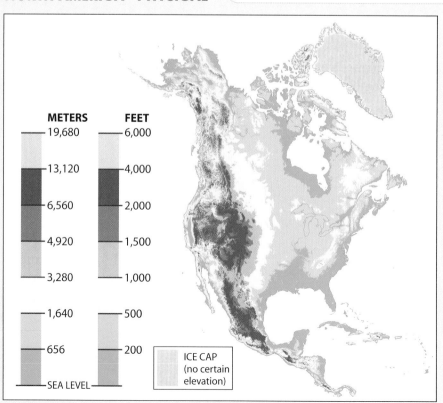

METERS	FEET
19,680	6,000
13,120	4,000
6,560	2,000
4,920	1,500
3,280	1,000
1,640	500
656	200
SEA LEVEL	

ICE CAP
(no certain
elevation)

RELIEF MAP OF CALIFORNIA

The lowest point in the Western Hemisphere is in Death Valley, California. It is 282 feet below sea level. Nearby is Mount Whitney, the highest mountain in the 48 contiguous states. It is 14,494 feet above sea level.

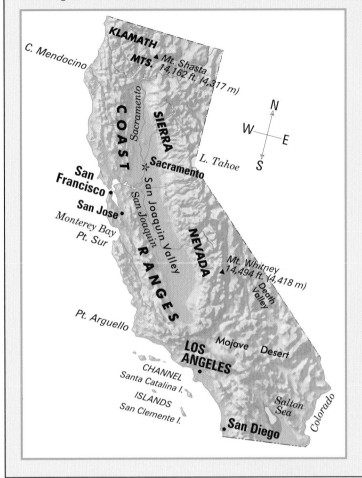

region, a plateau in the middle of the continent, is as high as the Appalachian Mountains. The Rocky Mountains are much higher, with elevations ranging from 5,000 to over 14,000 feet. Is North America's highest land in the East or in the West?

As you can see, some plateaus are as high as some mountains. So you cannot tell these land-forms apart on a color elevations map unless they are labeled.

Another way a map can show elevation is with lines and shading. On such a map, mountains look wrinkled. They are shown in **relief**, seeming to stand out from the lower lands around them. On a globe with raised relief, you can feel moun-tain ridges with your fingers.

The map of California on the left uses lines, shading and colors to show different elevations.

✷ Find California's largest valley. Is it in the middle of the state or near a border? Are the highest mountains in the east or west?

A third way mapmakers show elevation is by using **contour lines**. These lines connect points of equal elevation. The elevations may be written on the lines. When contour lines are close together the land is very steep.

✷ Look at the drawing on the left. Find the contour lines near the top of the mountain. Then look at the color key. What is the elevation of the land around the mountain peak?

CONTOUR MAP

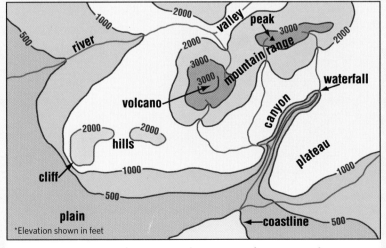

*Elevation shown in feet

METERS	Sea level to 150	150 to 300	300 to 600	600 to 900	Above 900
Sea level					
FEET	Sea level to 500	500 to 1000	1000 to 2000	2000 to 3000	Above 3000

THINK ABOUT IT

1. How can Pikes Peak have an elevation of 14,000 feet when it is only 7,500 feet above the ground?

2. How can you tell mountains and plateaus apart on a relief map? On a contour map?

3. Suppose you were planning a hike. How might a physical map help you?

29

DISTRIBUTION MAPS

LEADING PRODUCTS

OIL
URANIUM
TIMBER
OIL
IRON
LEAD & ZINC
OATS & BARLEY
FISH
IRON
NICKEL & COPPER
FISH
WHEAT
TIMBER
CORN
HOGS
COAL
VEGATABLES
URANIUM
WHEAT
LEAD
TOBACCO
FRUIT
COPPER
COTTON
CITRUS FRUIT
CATTLE
OIL
SUGARCANE
LEAD, ZINC & SILVER
SUGARCANE
OIL
BAUXITE
CORN
BANANAS

POPULATION

- CITIES WITH OVER 2,000,000 INHABITANTS (INCLUDING SUBURBS)

DENSITY PER		SQ. MI.	SQ. KM.	SQ. MI.	SQ. KM.
SQ. MI.	SQ. KM.	130 TO 260	50 TO 100	3 TO 25	1 TO 10
OVER 260	OVER 100	25 TO 130	10 TO 50	UNDER 3	UNDER 1

Maps can help you find people and things as well as places. A **distribution map** shows how people or things are spread out over an area.

One familiar kind of distribution map shows natural resources or products. A **natural resource** is anything in nature that people can use. Some resources are living things, such as plants and animals. Others are nonliving things found in or on the Earth, such as water and soil, coal and oil, gold and silver. People use resources for food, clothing, shelter, fuel and many other purposes.

Some resources are ready to use. Other resources are raw materials that are used to make finished goods.

✹ Look at the map of North America's leading products. Find two resources that are used as food. Find a resource that people use to make clothing.

A distribution map can also show you where people live. Every 10 years the United States counts the people in each city, town and village. This is called a **census**. The facts found in a census may be shown on a distribution map.

✹ Look at the **population map** of North America. It uses colors to show you which parts of the continent are crowded. Find the United States. Which part of our country is more crowded, the eastern half or the western half? Do more people live in the Northeast or the Northwest? Can you locate parts of North America where no one lives?

THINK ABOUT IT

Suppose you were going to live in another country. Would you want to know what resources it had and where they were? Why would this be helpful?

A very crowded, or densely populated, area has many people living close together. Would you expect to find many cities in such an area? Would you expect to find fewer cities in a less crowded, or sparsely populated, area? Why might people want to settle in or near a city?

A **vegetation map** is another kind of distribution map. **Vegetation** is plant life. Locate different regions on this vegetation map of North America.

Near the North Pole, the ground is always covered with thick ice. This cold **ice cap** is an area where no plants grow. South of the ice cap is the tundra and alpine region. Plants with deep roots cannot grow here. The **tundra** is a treeless plain where the soil beneath the surface stays frozen all year. In the spring and summer, moss and flowering plants appear. **Alpine** vegetation grows on high mountains. It is like the vegetation on the tundra. Wind and cold keep these plants from growing very tall. The **timberline** is the elevation above which trees cannot grow and only alpine plants are found.

Next comes the **forest** region, where there is enough rainfall for tall trees to grow. South of Canada's great forests are farmlands, grasslands and deserts. **Farmland** is flat, or rolling, with fertile soil and enough warmth and rainfall for crops to grow. A **grassland** region gets enough rain for grass, but not enough for tall trees. A **desert** is dry all year. Few plants can grow there.

✸ Find your part of the country on the vegetation map. Then locate that color in the map key. In what vegetation area do you live?

VEGETATION

VEGETATION

TROPICAL FOREST	MID-LATITUDE FOREST	MID-LATITUDE GRASSLAND
TROPICAL RAINFOREST	NEEDLELEAF FOREST	SHORT GRASS (STEPPE)
LIGHT TROPICAL FOREST	BROADLEAF FOREST	TALL GRASS (PRAIRIE)
TROPICAL GRASSLAND	MIXED NEEDLELEAF AND BROADLEAF FOREST	DESERT AND DESERT SHRUB
WOODED SAVANNA	WOODLAND AND SHRUB (MEDITERRANEAN)	TUNDRA AND ALPINE
		PERMANENT ICE COVER

THINK ABOUT IT

Compare the vegetation map on this page and the population map on the facing page. In what vegetation area are most of the very crowded lands? Why do you think this is so?

 PAST AND PRESENT

More than 200 years ago, in 1787, the founders of the United States drew up the Constitution. It is the basic law of the land. It says that every 10 years Congress must count the people. The more people a state has, the more representatives it can have in Congress.

The first United States census takers started work in 1790. They rode from place to place on horseback. In those days, there were fewer than 4 million Americans. Two hundred years later, in 1990, there were 249 million! The latest census was taken in 2000. When will the next census be?

ROAD MAPS

A **road map** shows roads and the towns and cities they connect. It tells you something about what these roads are like. It may also help you figure out driving distance between places.

Look at the symbols in the road map key below. Different symbols show different kinds of highways. The largest roads are **limited access** highways. They are often called expressways or freeways. They have special entrances and exits so traffic lights are not needed. Vehicles can safely move faster on these roads.

In the United States, many limited access highways are linked together in the **Interstate Highway** system. They are numbered to make it easier for drivers to know which road they are using.

Other highways also have numbers. They may be

Federal routes connecting states. These highways are also called U.S. routes. **State** routes connect places within one state. Still other roads may be county or local routes.

Road maps use different shapes, or **shields**, to identify route numbers for each type of road. Notice the different shields used on the map of southern Arizona below. What different highways are shown?

To find the road distance between places we must use a different method than measuring with a distance scale. Since roads bend and curve, a straight line distance doesn't tell us how far we must drive to get to a place.

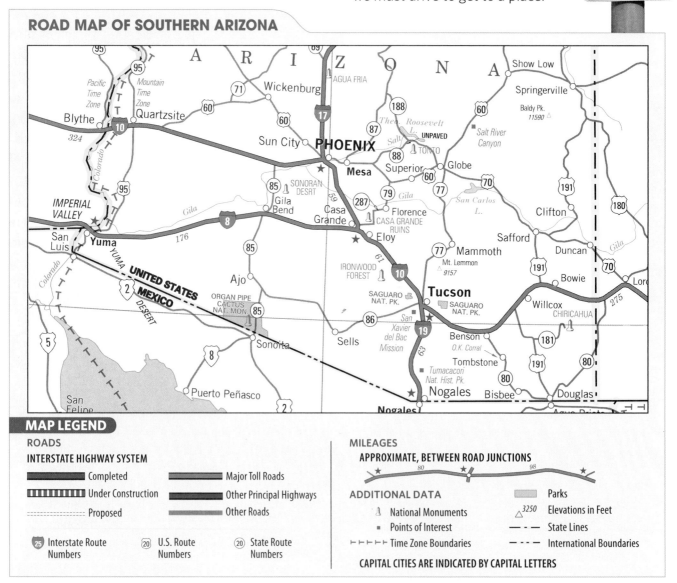

ROAD MAP OF SOUTHERN ARIZONA

MAP LEGEND

ROADS

INTERSTATE HIGHWAY SYSTEM

▬▬▬ Completed	▬▬▬ Major Toll Roads
▮▮▮▮▮ Under Construction	▬▬▬ Other Principal Highways
- - - - Proposed	▬▬▬ Other Roads

25 Interstate Route Numbers
20 U.S. Route Numbers
20 State Route Numbers

MILEAGES

APPROXIMATE, BETWEEN ROAD JUNCTIONS

★━━80━━━✦━━━98━━━★

ADDITIONAL DATA

⚐ National Monuments	▭ Parks
▪ Points of Interest	△3250 Elevations in Feet
⊢⊢⊢⊢⊢ Time Zone Boundaries	— · — State Lines
	— · · — International Boundaries

CAPITAL CITIES ARE INDICATED BY CAPITAL LETTERS

The road maps on these pages use numbers to show the mileage between stars. Find I-8 south of Phoenix. What is the mileage from Casa Grande west to Yuma?

The map below is a closeup road map of Tampa and St. Petersburg, Florida. It shows cities and their neighboring suburbs. Larger cities are shown in yellow.

✸ Let's learn to navigate using a road map. Try tracing routes. What Interstate highway would you take from Busch Gardens in Tampa to Sunken Gardens in St. Petersburg? What bridge would you use? What highway would you take from Tampa International Airport across the Gandy Bridge? Start at Tampa Airport again. Take U.S. Route 92 south for three miles to Interstate 275. Follow I-275 west to State Route 60. Follow Route 60 west to Clearwater. From Clearwater, what road would you take to St. Petersburg? What lake would you go by on the way there? What attractions could you visit in the St. Petersburg area?

💡 **THINK ABOUT IT**

If a local road ran for 30 miles between two towns, and an Interstate Highway was 32 miles between the same two towns, which would probably be the quickest way to get from one town to the other? Why?

Location and **movement** are two of geography's fundamental themes. Directions tell about **relative location**, or where one place is in relation to another. Latitude and longitude tell about **absolute location**, the fixed position of a place on our planet. Road maps show you ways to **move** from place to place. When people move, they carry their goods and ideas with them. They also see and learn many new things. Simply by traveling, people bring about change.

ROAD MAP OF TAMPA BAY

NAVIGATION BY SATELLITE

What is GPS?

Global **P**ositioning **S**ystem, or **GPS**, is a global system that uses signals transmitted by satellites that circle the Earth. The GPS receiver uses constant satellite signals to tell location, speed, direction, and time. A constellation of 24 NAVSTAR satellites and five ground stations is managed by the U.S. Air Force. Besides in-car navigation, GPS is used to study earthquakes, in telecommunication networks, for emergency services, and countless other ways to help our society.

How GPS Works for Cars

One of the uses for GPS is in-car navigation. **In-car navigation** is the process of guiding your car from one place to another. To use in-car navigation you need a GPS unit in the car. The GPS unit contains a map and location database. It receives extremely accurate information from satellites. The GPS unit receives four units of measurement from at least four satellites: **latitude**, **longitude, elevation** and **time**. Using geometry and trigonometry, the GPS unit turns the information into places on a map and shows a picture on the unit. The satellites continuously update the information.

Using In-Car Navigation

Planning a trip to visit friends, relatives, a vacation, or shopping is very easy using a GPS unit. Your unit can be installed in your car or be portable. Some hand-held devices such as wireless phones and computers have built-in GPS receivers, too.

To start your trip you will need to enter your starting address and the address you want to go to.

Your home, a street, a town, or any point of interest address can be the start or end points for your trip. The GPS unit receives satellite signals and figures out your location. Follow the voice or pictured directions from the GPS unit. The GPS unit will try to get you there in the shortest time or the fastest way.

✺ See the map on the left. The shortest way from your house to the mall passes the high school and turns at the post office towards the mall. The total distance from your house to the mall is 14 miles. It is 7 miles from home to the high school plus 4 miles to the post office and 3 more miles from the post office to the mall.

✺ The shortest way is not always the fastest. The fastest way from your house to the mall is by using highways 24 and 80. From your house get on highway 24, pass the train station and turn at the gas station onto highway 80 towards the mall. Most of the time using highways is faster than using local streets. How many more miles is it to the mall by highway?

Map

Home · Train Station · 24 · 6 · 4 · Gas Station · **Village** · 6 · 6 · 6 · 7 · High School · 8 · Fire Station · 7 · 80 · 2 · 4 · Movie Theater · 8 · Post Office · 3 · The Mall

Distance between points in miles

💡 THINK ABOUT IT

1. Using the sample map, what is the shortest distance from your home to the post office?

2. What is the fastest way from the mall to the gas station?

3. In your own home town, what is the shortest way from your house to your school? From your house to the library?

4. Can you think of other ways to use a GPS device? Discuss how GPS helps emergency services like fire and rescue.

For centuries, navigators and explorers have searched the heavens for a system that would help them to locate their position on Earth. About 4,000 years ago Phoenician sailors used basic charts and observations of the Sun and stars to guide their ships. Latitude can easily be determined using the sky to navigate. In the Northern Hemisphere, mariners could figure out the latitude by measuring the vertical distance of the North Star above the horizon. The vertical elevation is called altitude. The angle in degrees was the latitude of the ship's position.

However, longitude could only be estimated, at best. This was because the measurement of longitude is an East to West measurement made by comparing the difference between the time of day at the starting location and the new loca-tion. Even some of the best clocks of the early days could lose as much as 10 minutes per day, which translated into an error of 150 miles or more.

In 1957 the launch of the Sputnik satellite was the beginning of GPS. Scientists studying the orbit of the satellite realized they could track the satellite by its radio signal. This meant that a person could know his position on Earth if he could read the signal from the satellite, and at the same time he would know the exact location of the satellite in orbit. In 1964, U.S. submarines began using this method to figure out their location. One advancement in technology that made GPS possible was the development of the atomic clock. Atomic clocks are so precise that they measure time within a billionth of a second.

The United States government lets people use the system without charge for the public good. On June 26, 1993, the U.S. Air Force launched the 24th NAVSTAR satellite into orbit, completing a network of 24 satellites known as the Global Positioning System, or GPS. Since then, GPS has become a widely used aid to navigation worldwide, and a useful tool for map-making, land surveying, commerce and for scientific uses.

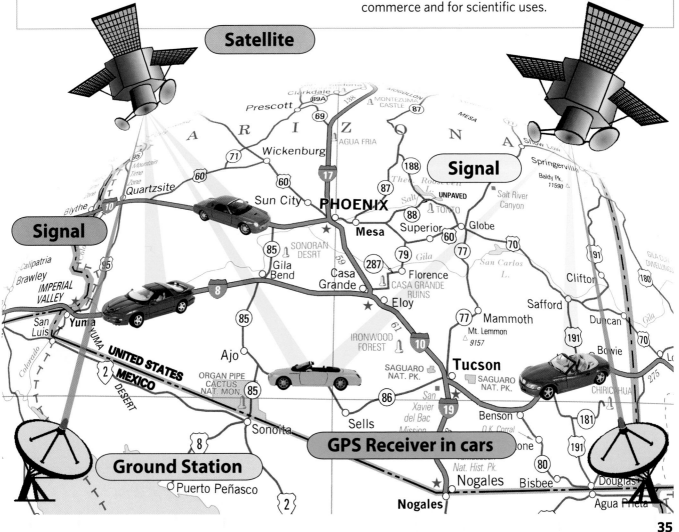

Satellite

Signal

Signal

GPS Receiver in cars

Ground Station

THE WORLD PHYSICAL

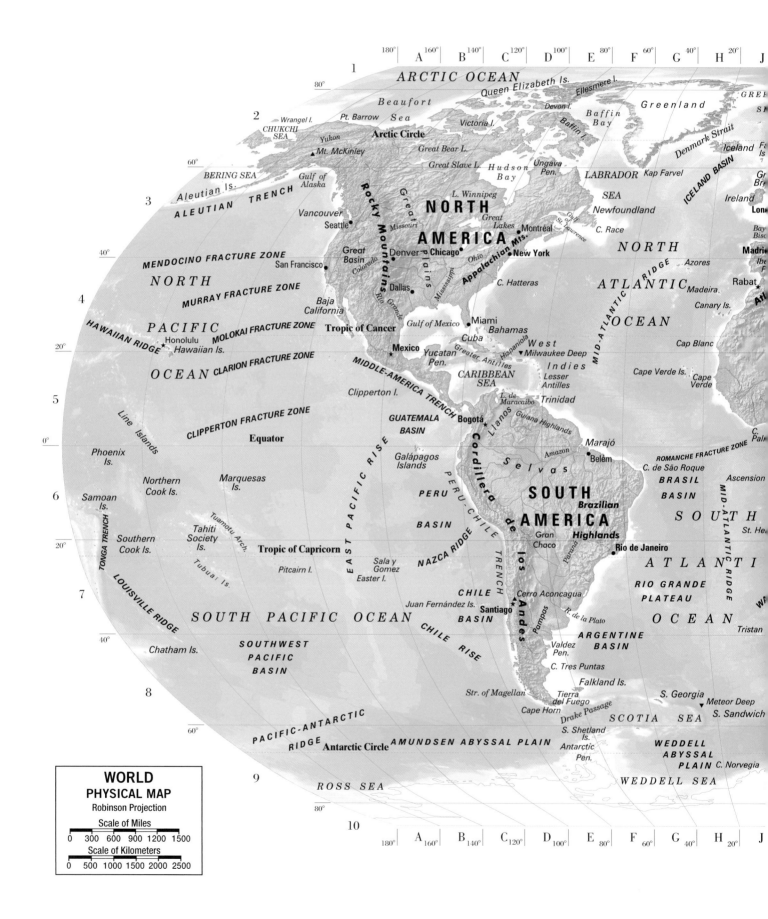

ARCTIC OCEAN

Queen Elizabeth Is.   Ellesmere I.

Beaufort   Devon I.   Baffin   Greenland
Sea   Victoria I.   Bay

Wrangel I.   Pt. Barrow   Baffin I.   Denmark Strait   Iceland
CHUKCHI   Arctic Circle   Ungava   Iceland Is.
SEA   Yukon   Great Bear L.   Hudson   Pen.   ICELAND BASIN
Mt. McKinley   Great Slave L.   Bay   LABRADOR   Kap Farvel   Ireland
BERING SEA   Gulf of   L. Winnipeg   SEA   Newfoundland
Aleutian Is.   Alaska   Rocky   Great Lakes   Montréal   C. Race   NORTH
ALEUTIAN TRENCH   Vancouver   Missouri   Gulf   St. Lawrence
Seattle   Mountains   NORTH   Great   Chicago   New York   ATLANTIC   Azores
MENDOCINO FRACTURE ZONE   AMERICA   Ohio   Appalachian Mts.   RIDGE   Madeira   Madrid
San Francisco   Great   Denver   Plains   C. Hatteras   OCEAN   Rabat
NORTH   Basin   Colorado   Mississippi   MID-ATLANTIC   Canary Is.
MURRAY FRACTURE ZONE   Dallas   Cap Blanc
Baja   Gulf of Mexico   Miami
PACIFIC   California   Tropic of Cancer   Bahamas
MOLOKAI FRACTURE ZONE   Honolulu   Cuba   West   Cape Verde Is.   Cape
HAWAIIAN RIDGE   Hawaiian Is.   Mexico   Yucatan   Greater Antilles   Milwaukee Deep   Verde
OCEAN   CLARION FRACTURE ZONE   Pen.   Hispaniola   Indies
CARIBBEAN   Lesser
SEA   Antilles
Clipperton I.   L. de   Trinidad
GUATEMALA   Maracaibo
Equator   BASIN   Bogotá   Guiana Highlands   ROMANCHE FRACTURE ZONE
CLIPPERTON FRACTURE ZONE   Llanos   Marajó   C. de São Roque
Phoenix   Galápagos   Amazon   Belém   BRASIL
Is.   Islands   Selvas   BASIN   Ascension
Northern   Marquesas   PERU-CHILE   SOUTH   Brazilian   SOUTH
Samoan   Cook Is.   Is.   BASIN   AMERICA   Highlands   St. He
Is.   Cordillera   Gran   Rio de Janeiro
Tahiti   Chaco   ATLANTI
Southern   Society   Tropic of Capricorn   de   Paraná
Cook Is.   Is.   NAZCA RIDGE   los   RIO GRANDE   OCEAN
Tubuai Is.   Pitcairn I.   Sala y   PLATEAU   Tristan
Gomez   Andes   Cerro Aconcagua
Easter I.   CHILE   Pampas   ARGENTINE
LOUISVILLE RIDGE   Juan Fernández Is.   Santiago   R. de la Plato   BASIN
Chatham Is.   SOUTH PACIFIC OCEAN   BASIN   CHILE RISE   Valdez   Tierra
SOUTHWEST   Pen.
PACIFIC   C. Tres Puntas   Falkland Is.
BASIN   Str. of Magellan   del Fuego   S. Georgia   Meteor Deep
Cape Horn   Drake Passage   SCOTIA   SEA   S. Sandwich
PACIFIC-ANTARCTIC   S. Shetland   WEDDELL
RIDGE   Antarctic Circle   AMUNDSEN ABYSSAL PLAIN   Is.   Antarctic   ABYSSAL
Pen.   PLAIN   C. Norvegia
ROSS SEA   WEDDELL SEA

WORLD
PHYSICAL MAP
Robinson Projection

Scale of Miles

| 0 | 300 | 600 | 900 | 1200 | 1500 |

Scale of Kilometers

| 0 | 500 | 1000 | 1500 | 2000 | 2500 |

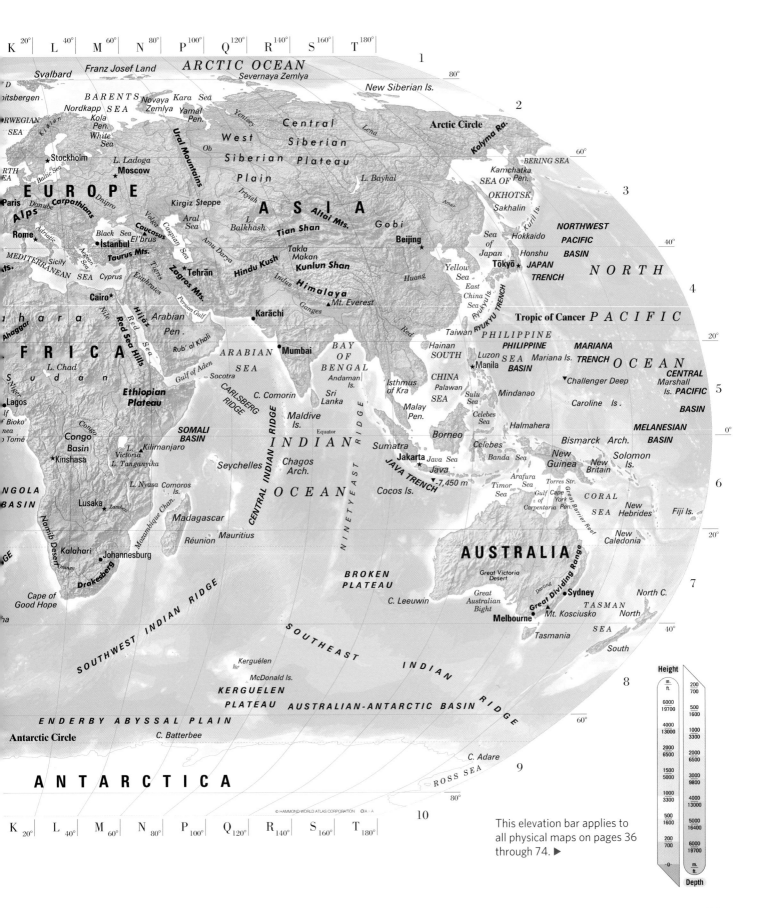

ARCTIC OCEAN

Svalbard Franz Josef Land Severnaya Zemlya New Siberian Is. 80°

itsbergen BARENTS Novaya Kara Sea Yamal Pen. 2

Nordkapp SEA Zemlya Yenisey Central Lena Arctic Circle Kolyma Ra. 60°

RWEGIAN Kola White Ob West Siberian Siberian Plateau BERING SEA

SEA Pen. Sea Plain L. Baykal Kamchatka SEA OF Sakhalin 3

Stockholm L. Ladoga Ural Mountains Irtysh Amur OKHOTSK Kuril Is. NORTHWEST

RTH Baltic Sea Moscow Kirgiz Steppe ASIA Gobi Hokkaido PACIFIC 40°

EA EUROPE Dnipro L. Altai Mts. Tian Shan Beijing Sea Honshu BASIN NORTH

Paris Danube Carpathians Volga Aral Balkhash of Tōkyō JAPAN 4

Alps Caucasus Caspian Sea Japan East TRENCH

Rome Adriatic Black Sea El'brus Takla Kunlun Shan Yellow China PACIFIC

Istanbul Taurus Mts. Makan Sea Sea Tropic of Cancer

MEDITERRANEAN Aegean Cyprus Zagros Mts. Tehrān Hindu Kush Himalaya Huang Ryukyu Is. 20°

ts. Sicily Sea Tigris Indus Ganges Mt. Everest Red Taiwan RYUKYU TRENCH PHILIPPINE

Cairo Nile Euphrates Persian Gulf PHILIPPINE MARIANA OCEAN

hara Red Hijaz Arabian SOUTH Luzon SEA Mariana Is. TRENCH

Ahaggar Red Sea Hills Pen. Rub' al Khali ARABIAN BAY CHINA Manila BASIN CENTRAL 5

FRICA Gulf of Aden SEA OF Andaman SEA Challenger Deep Marshall Is. PACIFIC

L. Chad Socotra C. Comorin BENGAL Is. Isthmus Palawan Mindanao Caroline Is. BASIN

Sudan Ethiopian CARLSBERG Sri of Kra Sulu Celebes MELANESIAN

Lagos Plateau RIDGE Maldive Lanka Malay Sea Halmahera Bismarck Arch. BASIN

Bioko SOMALI Is. Pen. Borneo Celebes New Solomon

nea Congo BASIN Equator Banda Sea Guinea Is.

Tomé Basin L. Kilimanjaro INDIAN Sumatra Java Sea New 0°

Congo Victoria Chagos JAVA TRENCH Jakarta Arafura Britain

Kinshasa L. Tanganyika Seychelles Arch. OCEAN Java Torres Str. Sea CORAL

L. Nyasa Comoros -7,450 m Cape SEA

NGOLA Lusaka Zambe Is. Cocos Is. of Gulf York New

BASIN Madagascar Mozambique Chan. Carpentaria Pen. Hebrides Fiji Is.

Mauritius Réunion AUSTRALIA New 20°

GE Namib Desert Kalahari BROKEN Great Victoria Great Barrier Reef Caledonia

Johannesburg PLATEAU Desert 7

Orange Drakesberg C. Leeuwin Great Sydney North C.

Cape of Australian Great Dividing Range TASMAN

Good Hope SOUTHWEST INDIAN RIDGE Bight Mt. Kosciusko North

ha Melbourne SEA

SOUTHEAST South 40°

Kerguélen INDIAN Tasmania

McDonald Is. RIDGE 8

KERGUELEN 60°

PLATEAU AUSTRALIAN-ANTARCTIC BASIN

ENDERBY ABYSSAL PLAIN

Antarctic Circle C. Batterbee

C. Adare 9

ROSS SEA

ANTARCTICA 80°

© HAMMOND WORLD ATLAS CORPORATION 10

CENTRAL INDIAN RIDGE NINETYEAST RIDGE

Height

m. ft.	
6000 19700	200 700
4000 13000	500 1600
2000 6500	1000 3300
1500 5000	2000 6500
1000 3300	3000 9800
500 1600	4000 13000
200 700	5000 16400
0	6000 19700
	m. ft.

Depth

This elevation bar applies to all physical maps on pages 36 through 74. ▶

THE WORLD POLITICAL

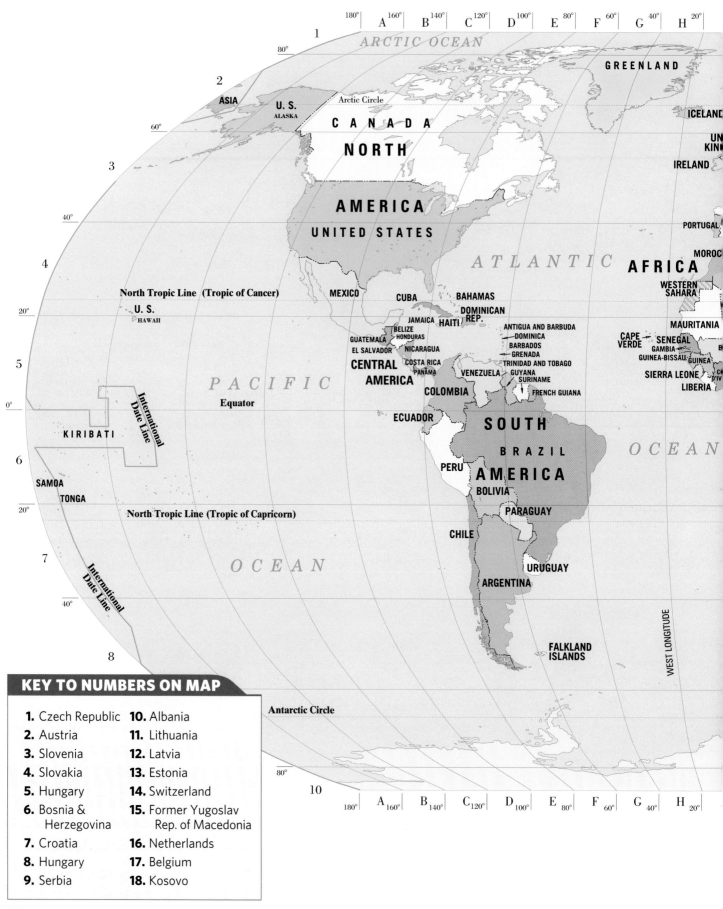

ARCTIC OCEAN

GREENLAND

ASIA

U.S. ALASKA

Arctic Circle

CANADA

NORTH

ICELAND

UN KIN

IRELAND

AMERICA

UNITED STATES

PORTUGAL

ATLANTIC

AFRICA

MOROC

MEXICO

North Tropic Line (Tropic of Cancer)

U.S. HAWAII

CUBA

BAHAMAS

WESTERN SAHARA

JAMAICA

DOMINICAN REP.

HAITI

ANTIGUA AND BARBUDA

BELIZE

DOMINICA

MAURITANIA

GUATEMALA

HONDURAS

BARBADOS

CAPE VERDE

SENEGAL

EL SALVADOR

NICARAGUA

GRENADA

GAMBIA

CENTRAL

COSTA RICA

TRINIDAD AND TOBAGO

GUINEA-BISSAU

GUINEA

AMERICA

PANAMA

VENEZUELA

GUYANA

SIERRA LEONE

C'D'IV

SURINAME

LIBERIA

COLOMBIA

FRENCH GUIANA

PACIFIC

Equator

ECUADOR

SOUTH

OCEAN

KIRIBATI

PERU

BRAZIL

AMERICA

BOLIVIA

SAMOA

TONGA

PARAGUAY

North Tropic Line (Tropic of Capricorn)

CHILE

OCEAN

URUGUAY

ARGENTINA

International Date Line

WEST LONGITUDE

FALKLAND ISLANDS

Antarctic Circle

KEY TO NUMBERS ON MAP

1. Czech Republic
2. Austria
3. Slovenia
4. Slovakia
5. Hungary
6. Bosnia & Herzegovina
7. Croatia
8. Hungary
9. Serbia
10. Albania
11. Lithuania
12. Latvia
13. Estonia
14. Switzerland
15. Former Yugoslav Rep. of Macedonia
16. Netherlands
17. Belgium
18. Kosovo

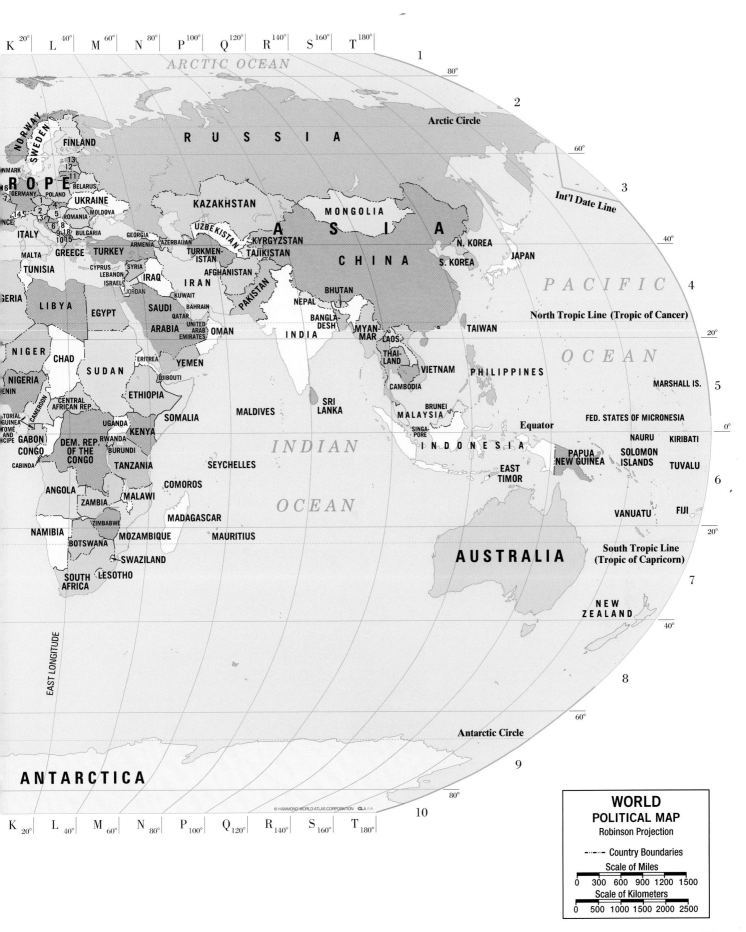

ARCTIC OCEAN

K 20° L 40° M 60° N 80° P 100° Q 120° R 140° S 160° T 180°

1

2

80°

Arctic Circle

60°

Int'l Date Line

3

NORWAY
SWEDEN
FINLAND
R U S S I A
NMARK
13
12
11
GERMANY
BELARUS
ROPE
POLAND
UKRAINE
KAZAKHSTAN
MONGOLIA
40°
NCE
14
2
ROMANIA
MOLDOVA
A S I A
ITALY
6
8
18
1
3
9
10 5
BULGARIA
GEORGIA
UZBEKISTAN
KYRGYZSTAN
CHINA
N. KOREA
JAPAN
4
GREECE
TURKEY
ARMENIA
AZERBAIJAN
TURKMEN-
ISTAN
TAJIKISTAN
S. KOREA
P A C I F I C
MALTA
CYPRUS
LEBANON
SYRIA
AFGHANISTAN
TUNISIA
IRAQ
IRAN
PAKISTAN
BHUTAN
TAIWAN
North Tropic Line (Tropic of Cancer)
ISRAEL
JORDAN
KUWAIT
NEPAL
20°
GERIA
LIBYA
EGYPT
SAUDI
ARABIA
BAHRAIN
QATAR
UNITED
ARAB
EMIRATES
OMAN
INDIA
BANGLA-
DESH
MYAN-
MAR
LAOS
THAI-
LAND
O C E A N
5
NIGER
CHAD
SUDAN
ERITREA
DJIBOUTI
YEMEN
VIETNAM
PHILIPPINES
MARSHALL IS.
NIGERIA
ENIN
CENTRAL
AFRICAN REP.
ETHIOPIA
SOMALIA
MALDIVES
SRI
LANKA
CAMBODIA
BRUNEI
MALAYSIA
FED. STATES OF MICRONESIA
TORIAL
GUINEA
OMÉ
AND
NCIPE
CAMEROON
UGANDA
KENYA
SINGA-
PORE
I N D O N E S I A
Equator
NAURU
KIRIBATI
0°
GABON
CONGO
DEM. REP.
OF THE
CONGO
RWANDA
BURUNDI
I N D I A N
SEYCHELLES
PAPUA
NEW GUINEA
SOLOMON
ISLANDS
TUVALU
CABINDA
TANZANIA
EAST
TIMOR
6
ANGOLA
MALAWI
COMOROS
O C E A N
FIJI
ZAMBIA
MADAGASCAR
VANUATU
ZIMBABWE
MOZAMBIQUE
MAURITIUS
20°
NAMIBIA
BOTSWANA
SWAZILAND
AUSTRALIA
South Tropic Line
(Tropic of Capricorn)
7
SOUTH
AFRICA
LESOTHO
N E W
Z E A L A N D
40°

EAST LONGITUDE

8

60°

Antarctic Circle

9

A N T A R C T I C A

80°

© HAMMOND WORLD ATLAS CORPORATION **CL** A A A

10

K 20° L 40° M 60° N 80° P 100° Q 120° R 140° S 160° T 180°

WORLD
POLITICAL MAP
Robinson Projection

–·–·– Country Boundaries
Scale of Miles
0   300   600   900   1200   1500
Scale of Kilometers
0   500   1000   1500   2000   2500

NORTH AMERICA OUR CONTINENT

Grizzly Bear

North America is the Earth's third-largest continent. Three of the world's four oceans border North America. Our continent joins South America at the narrow Isthmus of Panama. There, the Panama Canal connects the Atlantic and Pacific Oceans.

North America's size gives it a wide range of climates. Near the Arctic Ocean in the north, it is always cold. In the far south, it is always hot, except at high elevations. In between, a wide area of temperate climate has hot summers and cold winters.

Great seas, gulfs and bays cut into the mainland. Many peninsulas extend from the mainland. These features give North America the longest coastline of any continent. Many good harbors are found here.

North America has two major mountain systems. The rugged Rocky Mountains in the west and the Appalachian Mountains in the east rise on the edges of a vast central plain. Twin mountain ranges run down the Pacific coast.

East of these coast ranges is an arid plateau that stretches to the base of the Rocky Mountains. The Grand Canyon of the Colorado River is here. North America's largest deserts are also found here.

In Mexico, most of the people live on a high plateau between mountains. The climate here is cooler than on the coasts.

Look at the physical map on page 42. You can see the low coastal plains which border the Atlantic Ocean and the Gulf of Mexico. West of the Appalachian Mountains are interior plains drained by lengthy rivers.

Now look at the population map of North America on the next page. The most crowded region is in the eastern United States. This area is just south of the Great Lakes, the largest freshwater lakes in the world. People like to settle on flat, fertile land near good waterways.

Ten nations are located on the mainland of North America. Canada, the United States and Mexico take up most of the continent's land. Seven smaller countries lie between Mexico and South America. Find their names on the map on page 43. This area is called Central America. Still other nations are found on the islands of the Caribbean Sea.

The first Americans crossed from northeast Asia to Alaska thousands of years ago. These people were the ancestors of Native Americans, or American Indians. Much later, Europeans explored the continent and settled here. Today, Spanish, English and French are spoken and many of the customs and ideas they brought here are reflected around us.

CONTINENT CLOSEUP

- Mammoth Cave in Kentucky is the Earth's largest, with 300 miles of passages.

- A dozen island nations border the Caribbean Sea. Cuba is the largest. Many other islands are governed by nations outside the region.

- Canada has the longest coastline of any country in the world.

- At the Bering Strait, North America is only 2-1/2 miles from Asia.

▼North America has many large national parks, including Arches National Park in Utah.

● CITIES WITH OVER 2,000,000
INHABITANTS (INCLUDING SUBURBS)

POPULATION DISTRIBUTION

DENSITY PER		SQ. MI.	SQ. KM.		SQ. MI.	SQ. KM.
SQ. MI.	SQ. KM.	130 TO 260	50 TO 100		3 TO 25	1 TO 10
OVER 260	OVER 100	25 TO 130	10 TO 50		UNDER 3	UNDER 1

LAND USE

CEREALS, LIVESTOCK	COTTON & SPECIAL CROPS
LIVESTOCK RANCHING & LIMITED AGRICULTURE	DIVERSIFIED TROPICAL CROPS
FRUIT, TRUCK & MIXED FARMING	GENERAL FARMING

DAIRY

FORESTS

UNPRODUCTIVE

CLIMATE

HUMID TROPICAL
- Af NO DRY SEASON
- Am SHORT DRY SEASON
- Aw DRY WINTER

DRY
- BS SEMIARID ⎤ h HOT
- BW ARID   ⎦ k COLD

HUMID WARM
- Cf NO DRY SEASON
- Cw DRY WINTER
- Cs DRY SUMMER

HUMID COLD
- Df NO DRY SEASON
- Ds DRY SUMMER

COLD POLAR
- ET SHORT COOL SUMMER, LONG COLD WINTER
- EF PERPETUAL FROST

a HOT SUMMER
b COOL SUMMER
c SHORT COOL SUMMER

AFTER KOEPPEN-GEIGER

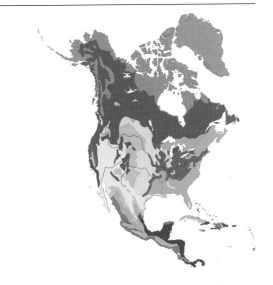

VEGETATION

TROPICAL FOREST
- TROPICAL RAINFOREST
- LIGHT TROPICAL FOREST

TROPICAL GRASSLAND
- WOODED SAVANNA

MID-LATITUDE FOREST
- NEEDLELEAF FOREST
- BROADLEAF FOREST
- MIXED NEEDLELEAF AND BROADLEAF FOREST
- WOODLAND AND SHRUB (MEDITERRANEAN)

MID-LATITUDE GRASSLAND
- SHORT GRASS (STEPPE)
- TALL GRASS (PRAIRIE)
- DESERT AND DESERT SHRUB
- TUNDRA AND ALPINE
- PERMANENT ICE COVER

▼ Boston, Massachusetts is one of many large cities in North America.

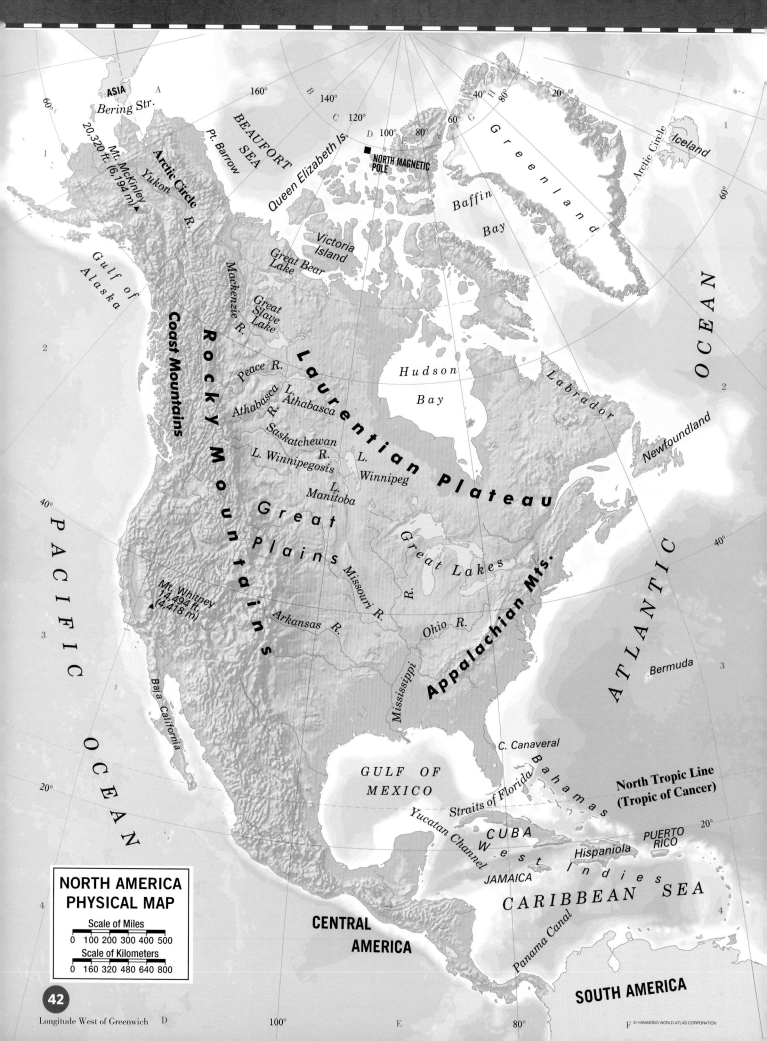

ASIA
Bering Str.
Mt. McKinley
20,320 ft. (6,194 m)▲
Yukon
Arctic Circle
Pt. Barrow
BEAUFORT
SEA
60°
A
160°
B
140°
C
120°
D
100°
E
80°
F
60°
G
40°
H
80°
20°
Arctic Circle
Iceland
1
1

Queen Elizabeth Is.
NORTH MAGNETIC
POLE
Greenland
Gulf of
Alaska
Mackenzie R.
Victoria
Island
Great Bear
Lake
Baffin
Bay
60°

Coast Mountains
Great
Slave
Lake
Rocky Mountains
Peace R.
Athabasca
R.
Athabasca
L.
Hudson
Bay
Labrador
2
2

Saskatchewan
R.
L. Winnipegosis
L.
Manitoba
L.
Winnipeg
Laurentian Plateau
Newfoundland

PACIFIC
40°
Great
Plains
Great Lakes
Appalachian Mts.
40°

Mt. Whitney
14,494 ft.
(4,418 m)▲
Arkansas R.
Missouri R.
Ohio R.
ATLANTIC
Bermuda
3
3

Baja California
Mississippi
OCEAN

OCEAN
20°
GULF OF
MEXICO
C. Canaveral
Bahamas
North Tropic Line
(Tropic of Cancer)
20°

Straits of Florida
Yucatan Channel
CUBA
West Indies
PUERTO
RICO
Hispaniola
JAMAICA
CARIBBEAN SEA
4

NORTH AMERICA
PHYSICAL MAP

Scale of Miles
0 100 200 300 400 500

Scale of Kilometers
0 160 320 480 640 800

CENTRAL
AMERICA
Panama Canal

SOUTH AMERICA

42

Longitude West of Greenwich   D

100°   E   80°   F © HAMMOND WORLD ATLAS CORPORATION

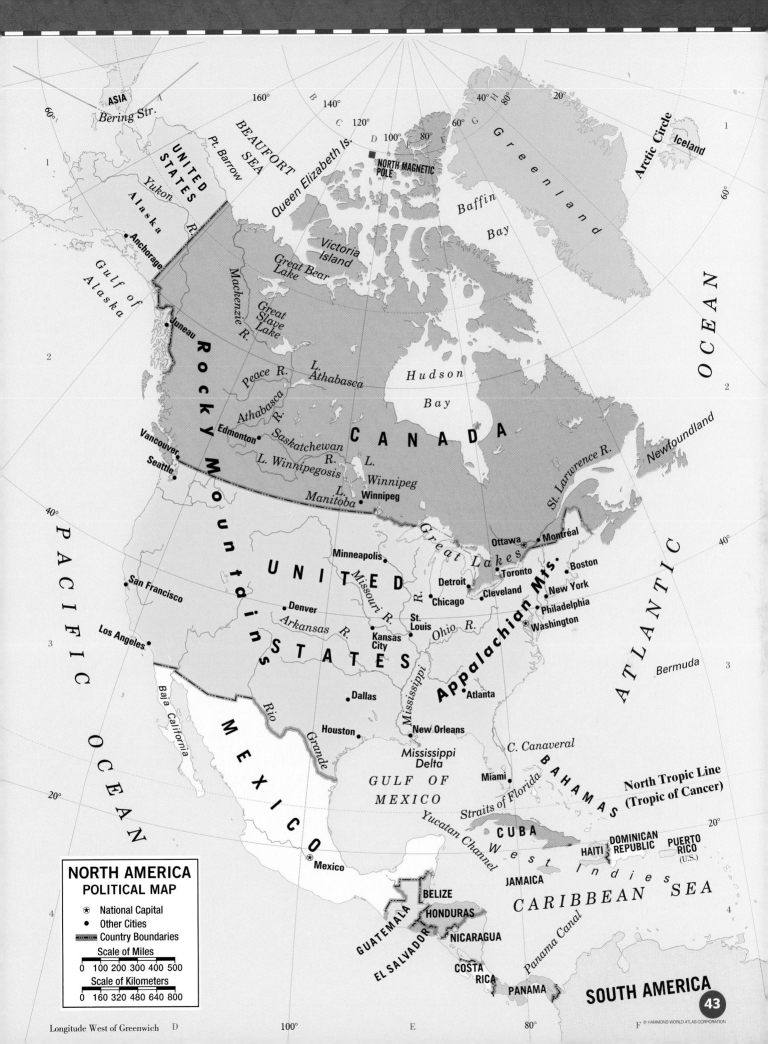

NORTH AMERICA POLITICAL MAP

ASIA
Bering Str.

BEAUFORT SEA
Pt. Barrow

UNITED STATES
Yukon
Alaska
Anchorage

Gulf of Alaska
Juneau

Queen Elizabeth Is.

NORTH MAGNETIC POLE

Greenland

Baffin Bay

Arctic Circle
Iceland

Victoria Island

Great Bear Lake

Mackenzie R.

Great Slave Lake

Peace R.

L. Athabasca

Athabasca R.

Edmonton

Saskatchewan R.

L. Winnipegosis

L. Manitoba

L. Winnipeg

Winnipeg

Hudson Bay

CANADA

Rocky Mountains

Vancouver
Seattle

Ottawa
Montréal

Minneapolis

Great Lakes

Toronto
Detroit
Cleveland
Chicago

Boston
New York
Philadelphia
Washington

St. Larwrence R.

Newfoundland

San Francisco

UNITED STATES

Missouri R.

Denver

Arkansas R.

Kansas City

St. Louis

Ohio R.

Appalachian Mts.

Los Angeles

Dallas

Mississippi R.

Atlanta

Bermuda

Baja California

Rio Grande

MEXICO

Houston

New Orleans

Mississippi Delta

GULF OF MEXICO

Miami

C. Canaveral

BAHAMAS

North Tropic Line
(Tropic of Cancer)

Mexico

Straits of Florida

Yucatan Channel

CUBA

West Indies

DOMINICAN REPUBLIC

HAITI

PUERTO RICO
(U.S.)

JAMAICA

CARIBBEAN SEA

BELIZE

GUATEMALA

HONDURAS

EL SALVADOR

NICARAGUA

COSTA RICA

PANAMA

Panama Canal

SOUTH AMERICA

PACIFIC OCEAN

ATLANTIC OCEAN

NORTH AMERICA
POLITICAL MAP
⊛ National Capital
• Other Cities
▬ Country Boundaries
Scale of Miles
0 100 200 300 400 500
Scale of Kilometers
0 160 320 480 640 800

Longitude West of Greenwich

© HAMMOND WORLD ATLAS CORPORATION

43

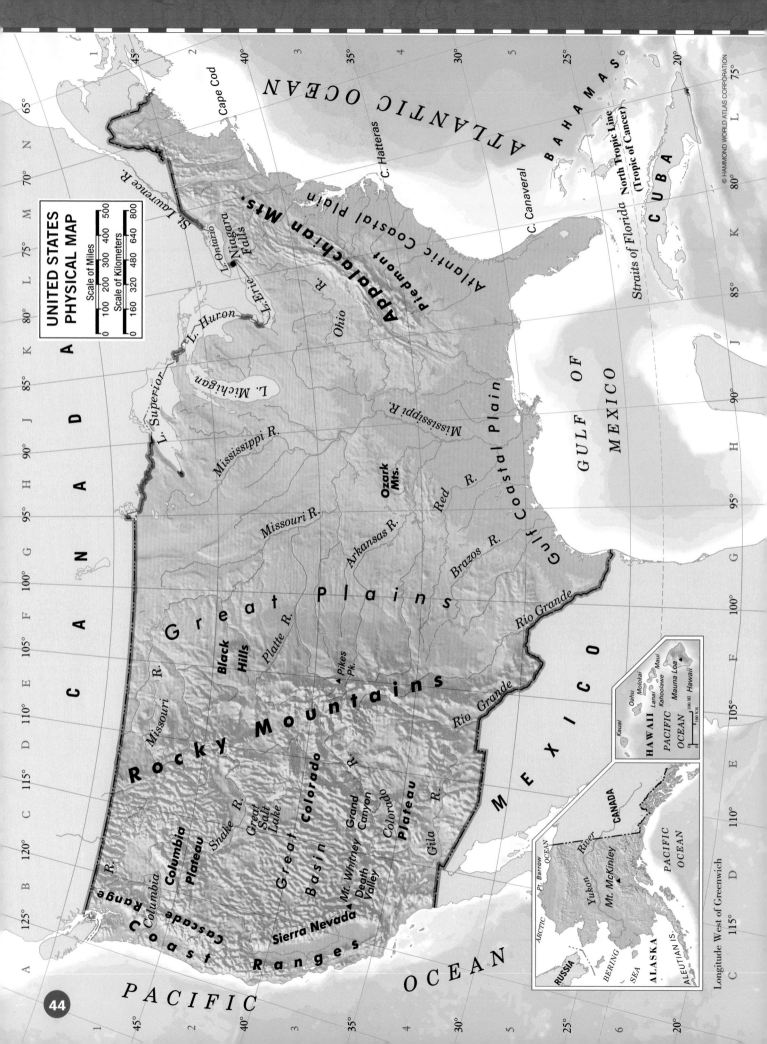

UNITED STATES PHYSICAL MAP

Scale of Miles
0 100 200 300 400 500

Scale of Kilometers
0 160 320 480 640 800

PACIFIC OCEAN

ATLANTIC OCEAN

GULF OF MEXICO

CANADA

MEXICO

CUBA

BAHAMAS

Cape Cod

C. Hatteras

C. Canaveral

Straits of Florida

North Tropic Line
(Tropic of Cancer)

St. Lawrence R.

L. Ontario

Niagara Falls

L. Erie

L. Huron

L. Michigan

L. Superior

Ohio R.

Mississippi R.

Missouri R.

Mississippi R.

Arkansas R.

Red R.

Brazos R.

Rio Grande

Rio Grande

Rio Grande

Platte R.

Colorado R.

Gila R.

Snake R.

Missouri R.

Columbia R.

Ozark Mts.

Appalachian Mts.

Piedmont

Atlantic Coastal Plain

Gulf Coastal Plain

Great Plains

Rocky Mountains

Black Hills

▲ Pikes Pk.

Great Basin

Great Salt Lake

Colorado Plateau

Grand Canyon

Columbia Plateau

Cascade Range

Coast Ranges

Sierra Nevada

▲ Mt. Whitney

Death Valley

HAWAII
Kauai
Oahu
Molokai
Lanai
Maui
Kahoolawe
Mauna Loa ▲
Hawaii

PACIFIC OCEAN

0 100 MI
0 100 KM

ALASKA
RUSSIA
BERING SEA
ARCTIC OCEAN
Pt. Barrow
Yukon River
CANADA
PACIFIC OCEAN
▲ Mt. McKinley
ALEUTIAN IS.

Longitude West of Greenwich

© HAMMOND WORLD ATLAS CORPORATION

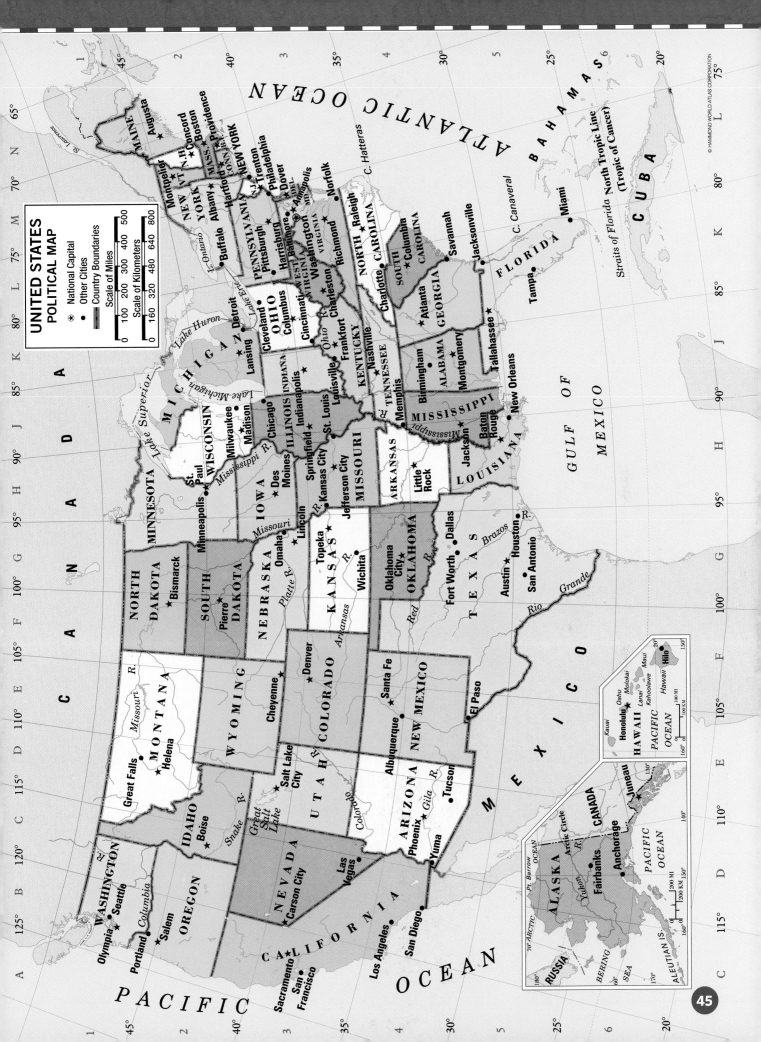

UNITED STATES POLITICAL MAP

⊛ National Capital
● Other Cities
▬▬ Country Boundaries

Scale of Miles
0 100 200 300 400 500

Scale of Kilometers
0 160 320 480 640 800

ATLANTIC OCEAN

BAHAMAS

CUBA

North Tropic Line (Tropic of Cancer)

Straits of Florida

C. Canaveral

C. Hatteras

MAINE
Augusta ★

Montpelier ★ CONCORD
VT. N.H.
Boston ★ MASS.
Providence
Hartford CONN.
Albany ● NEW YORK
Buffalo ●
Trenton N.J.
Philadelphia
Dover DEL.
Annapolis
Norfolk ●
Richmond ★ VIRGINIA

Montpelier
NEW YORK
L. Ontario
Lake Erie

PENNSYLVANIA
Pittsburgh ●
Harrisburg ★
WEST VIRGINIA
Washington
Baltimore ●
Charleston ★
Raleigh ★
NORTH CAROLINA
Charlotte ●

Lansing ★
Detroit ●
MICHIGAN

Lake Huron
Lake Superior
Lake Michigan

Cleveland ●
OHIO
Columbus ★
Cincinnati ●
INDIANA
Frankfort ★
KENTUCKY
Nashville ★
TENNESSEE
Memphis ●

Columbia ★
SOUTH CAROLINA
Savannah ●
Jacksonville ●
Atlanta ★
GEORGIA
FLORIDA
ALABAMA
Montgomery ★
Tallahassee ★
Birmingham ●
Tampa ●
Miami ●

New Orleans ●
Baton Rouge ★
Jackson ★
MISSISSIPPI
LOUISIANA

Mississippi R.

GULF OF MEXICO

CANADA
St. Lawrence

St. Paul ★
Minneapolis ●
WISCONSIN
Madison ★
Milwaukee ●
MINNESOTA
Chicago ●
ILLINOIS
Springfield ★
St. Louis ●
Indianapolis ★
Louisville ●
Ohio R.

IOWA
Des Moines ★
Lincoln ★
Omaha ●
NEBRASKA

Missouri R.
Platte R.

MISSOURI
Jefferson City ★
Kansas City ●
Topeka ★
KANSAS
Wichita ●

ARKANSAS
Little Rock ★
Mississippi R.

NORTH DAKOTA
Bismarck ★

SOUTH DAKOTA
Pierre ★

Dallas ●
Fort Worth ●
Brazos R.
Red R.
Arkansas R.

OKLAHOMA
Oklahoma City ★

TEXAS
Austin ★
San Antonio ●
Houston ●

Rio Grande

El Paso ●

MEXICO

Denver ★
COLORADO
Cheyenne ★
WYOMING

Santa Fe ★
NEW MEXICO
Albuquerque ●

Missouri R.

MONTANA
Helena ★
Great Falls ●

IDAHO
Boise ★
Snake R.

Salt Lake City ●
UTAH
Great Salt Lake
Colorado R.

Phoenix ★
ARIZONA
Tucson ●
Gila R.
Yuma ●

NEVADA
Carson City ★
Las Vegas ●

WASHINGTON
Olympia ★
Seattle ●
Columbia R.

OREGON
Portland ●
Salem ★

Sacramento ★
San Francisco ●
CALIFORNIA
Los Angeles ●
San Diego ●

PACIFIC OCEAN

© HAMMOND WORLD ATLAS CORPORATION

Hawaii inset

PACIFIC OCEAN
HAWAII
Kauai
Oahu Honolulu
Molokai
Lanai Maui
Kahoolawe
Hawaii Hilo

0 100 MI
0 100 KM

Alaska inset

ALASKA
CANADA
Juneau
Anchorage
Fairbanks
Pt. Barrow
Arctic Circle
Yukon R.
RUSSIA
BERING SEA
ALEUTIAN IS.
PACIFIC OCEAN

0 200 MI
0 200 KM

45

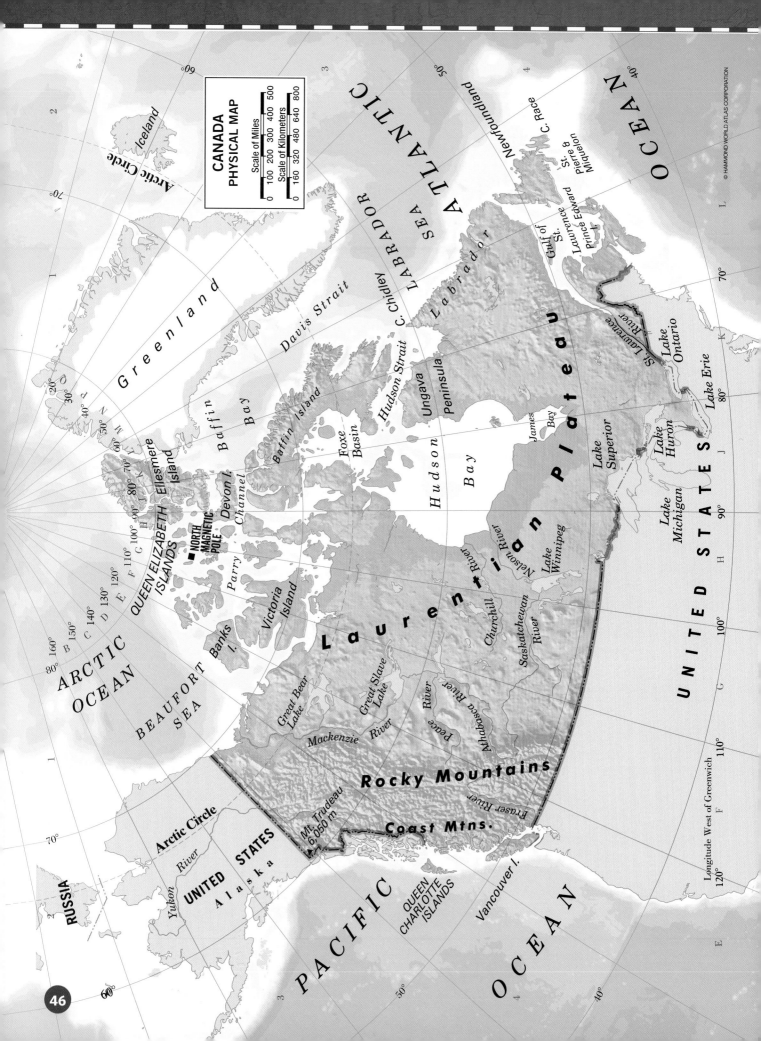

CANADA PHYSICAL MAP

Scale of Miles
0 100 200 300 400 500

Scale of Kilometers
0 160 320 480 640 800

ATLANTIC OCEAN

PACIFIC OCEAN

ARCTIC OCEAN

BEAUFORT SEA

LABRADOR SEA

Davis Strait

Baffin Bay

Greenland

Iceland

Arctic Circle

RUSSIA

UNITED STATES
Alaska

Yukon River

Queen Charlotte Islands

Vancouver I.

Coast Mtns.

Fraser River

Rocky Mountains

Mt. Trudeau
6,050 m

Mackenzie River

Peace River

Athabasca River

Great Bear Lake

Great Slave Lake

Banks I.

Victoria Island

Parry Channel

Devon I.

Ellesmere Island

QUEEN ELIZABETH ISLANDS

NORTH MAGNETIC POLE

Baffin Island

Foxe Basin

Hudson Strait

C. Chidley

Ungava Peninsula

Hudson Bay

James Bay

Laurentian Plateau

Labrador

Newfoundland

C. Race

St. & Pierre Miquelon

Gulf of St. Lawrence

Prince Edward I.

St. Lawrence River

Lake Ontario

Lake Erie

Lake Huron

Lake Michigan

Lake Superior

Lake Winnipeg

Nelson River

Churchill River

Saskatchewan River

UNITED STATES

Longitude West of Greenwich

© HAMMOND WORLD ATLAS CORPORATION

46

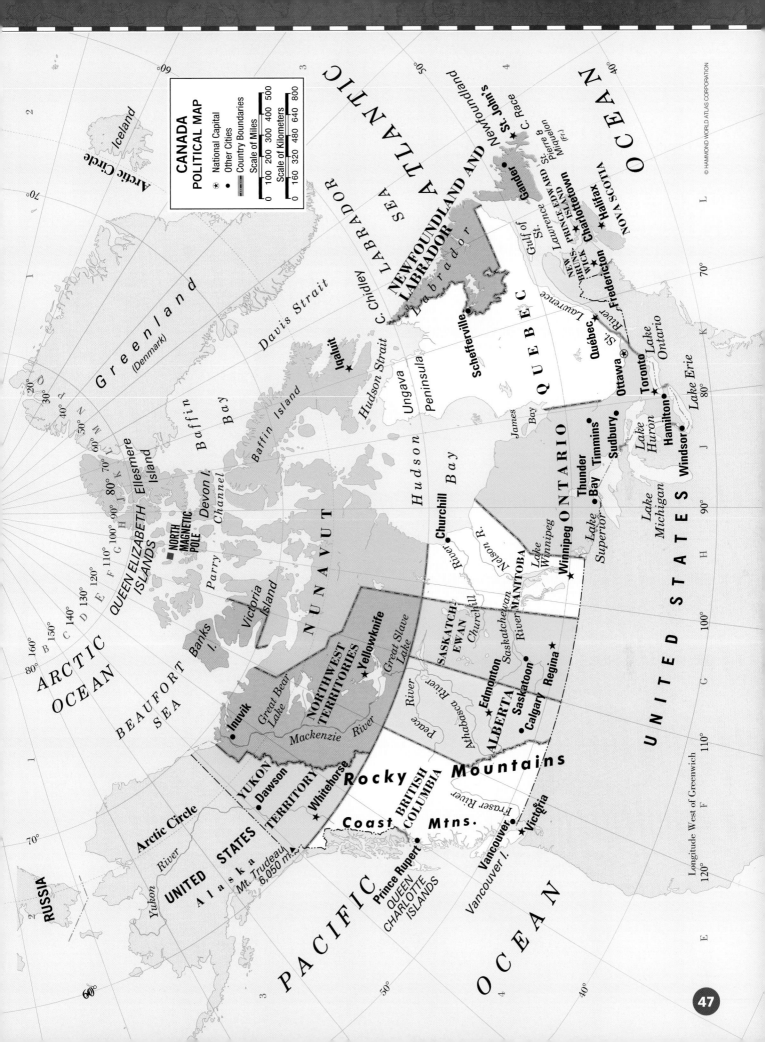

CANADA POLITICAL MAP

★ National Capital
● Other Cities
— Country Boundaries

Scale of Miles
0 100 200 300 400 500

Scale of Kilometers
0 160 320 480 640 800

© HAMMOND WORLD ATLAS CORPORATION

Iceland

Arctic Circle

Greenland
(Denmark)

ATLANTIC OCEAN

Newfoundland
★ **St. John's**
C. Race
St. Pierre & Miquelon (Fr.)
● **Gander**

Davis Strait

C. Chidley

NEWFOUNDLAND AND LABRADOR

Labrador

PRINCE EDWARD ISLAND
★ **Charlottetown**
Halifax
NOVA SCOTIA

Gulf of St. Lawrence

NEW BRUNS- WICK
★ **Fredericton**

Baffin Bay

Baffin Island

★ **Iqaluit**

Hudson Strait

Ungava Peninsula

QUEBEC

St. Lawrence River

● **Schefferville**

● **Québec**
★ **Ottawa** ⊛
Toronto
Lake Ontario
Hamilton
Lake Erie
Windsor

Devon I.
Parry Channel
Ellesmere Island
QUEEN ELIZABETH ISLANDS

NORTH MAGNETIC POLE

Victoria Island

NUNAVUT

James Bay

Hudson Bay

● **Churchill**

Churchill River

Nelson R.

ONTARIO
● **Thunder Bay**
● **Timmins**
● **Sudbury**
Lake Superior
Lake Huron
Lake Michigan

Winnipeg ★
MANITOBA
Lake Winnipeg

ARCTIC OCEAN

Banks I.

BEAUFORT SEA

Great Bear Lake

NORTHWEST TERRITORIES
★ **Yellowknife**
Great Slave Lake

Mackenzie River

● **Inuvik**

SASKATCHEWAN

Athabasca River
Saskatchewan River

● **Edmonton**
● **Saskatoon**
Regina ★

ALBERTA
● **Calgary**

Peace River

UNITED STATES

Yukon River

RUSSIA

Arctic Circle

UNITED STATES
Alaska

YUKON TERRITORY
● **Dawson**
★ **Whitehorse**

Rocky Mountains

BRITISH COLUMBIA
Fraser River

Coast Mtns.

△ **Mt. Trudeau 6,050 m.**

Prince Rupert ●
QUEEN CHARLOTTE ISLANDS

Vancouver
★ **Victoria**
Vancouver I.

PACIFIC OCEAN

UNITED STATES

Longitude West of Greenwich

47

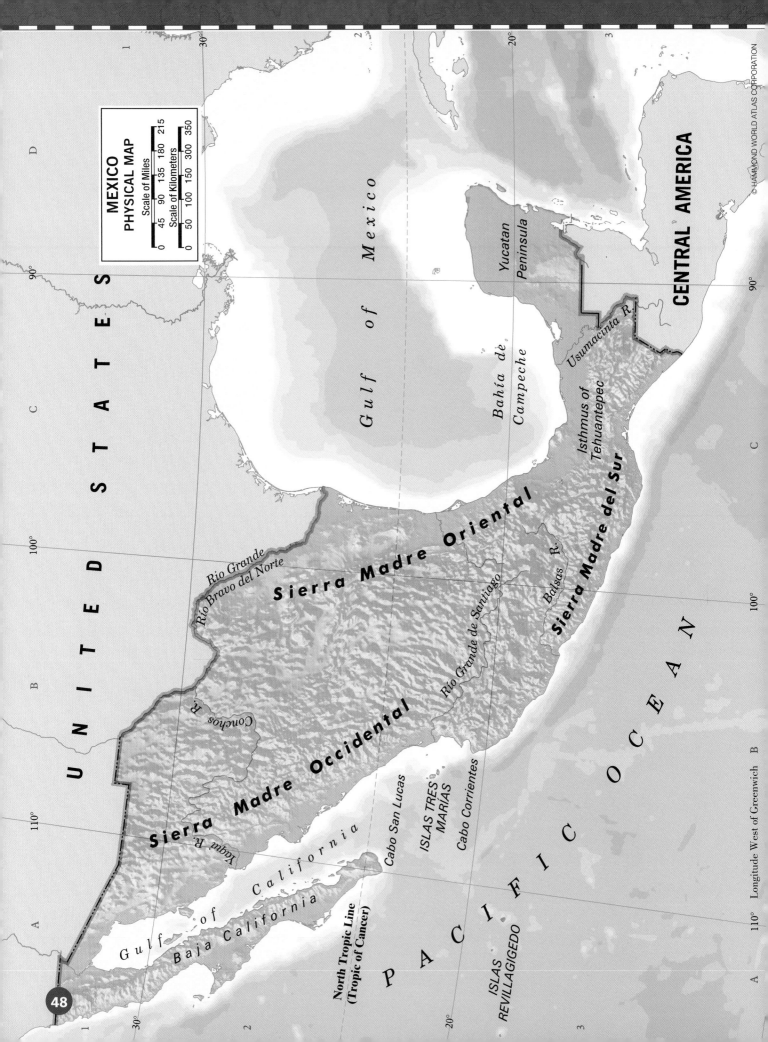

MEXICO
PHYSICAL MAP

Scale of Miles
0   45   90   135   180   215

Scale of Kilometers
0   50   100   150   300   350

UNITED STATES

Gulf of Mexico

Yucatan Peninsula

Bahía de Campeche

CENTRAL AMERICA

Usumacinta R.

Isthmus of Tehuantepec

Rio Grande
Río Bravo del Norte

Sierra Madre Oriental

Sierra Madre del Sur

Conchos R.

Sierra Madre Occidental

Río Grande de Santiago

Balsas R.

PACIFIC OCEAN

Yaqui R.

Gulf of California

Baja California

Cabo San Lucas

ISLAS TRES MARÍAS

Cabo Corrientes

North Tropic Line
(Tropic of Cancer)

ISLAS REVILLAGIGEDO

Longitude West of Greenwich

© HAMMOND WORLD ATLAS CORPORATION

MEXICO POLITICAL MAP

⊛ National Capital
● Other Cities
‥‥‥ Country Boundaries

Scale of Miles
0 45 90 135 180 215

Scale of Kilometers
0 50 100 150 300 350

UNITED STATES

CENTRAL AMERICA

Gulf of Mexico

Bahía de Campeche

PACIFIC OCEAN

Gulf of California

Mexicali ★
Tijuana ●

Ciudad Juárez ●

Hermosillo ●

La Paz ★

Mazatlán ●

Tepic ★

Guadalajara ★

Colima ●

Chihuahua ●

Hidalgo del Parral ●

Durango ●

Culiacán Rosales ★

Piedras Negras ●

Saltillo ★

Torreón ●

Zacatecas ★

Aguascalientes ★

Guanajuato ★

Morelia ●

Nuevo Laredo ●

Monterrey ★

San Luis Potosí ★

Querétaro ★

Toluca ★
México ⊛
Cuernavaca ★
Pachuca ★
Tlaxcala
Puebla ★

Matamoros ●

Ciudad Victoria ★

Tampico ●

Jalapa ★
Veracruz ●

Villahermosa ★

Campeche ★

Mérida ★

Cancún ●

Chetumal ★

Tuxtla Gutiérrez ★

Oaxaca ★

Chilpancingo ★

Acapulco ●

BAJA CALIFORNIA

BAJA CALIFORNIA SUR

SONORA

CHIHUAHUA

SINALOA

DURANGO

COAHUILA DE ZARAGOZA

NUEVO LEÓN

TAMAULIPAS

ZACATECAS

NAYARIT

JALISCO

COLIMA

**AGUAS-
CALIENTES**

SAN LUIS POTOSÍ

**GUANA-
JUATO**

QUERÉTARO DE ARTEAGA

HIDALGO

MICHOACÁN DE OCAMPO

MÉXICO
MORELOS
TLAXCALA
PUEBLA

**VERACRUZ-
LLAVE**

GUERRERO

OAXACA

TABASCO

CHIAPAS

CAMPECHE

YUCATÁN

QUINTANA ROO

Río Bravos del Norte
Rio Grande

Conchos R.

Yaqui R.

Cabo San Lucas

Cabo Corrientes

ISLAS TRES MARÍAS

ISLAS REVILLAGIGEDO

Isthmus of Tehuantepec

North Tropic Line
(Tropic of Cancer)

110° Longitude West of Greenwich

100°

90°

30°

20°

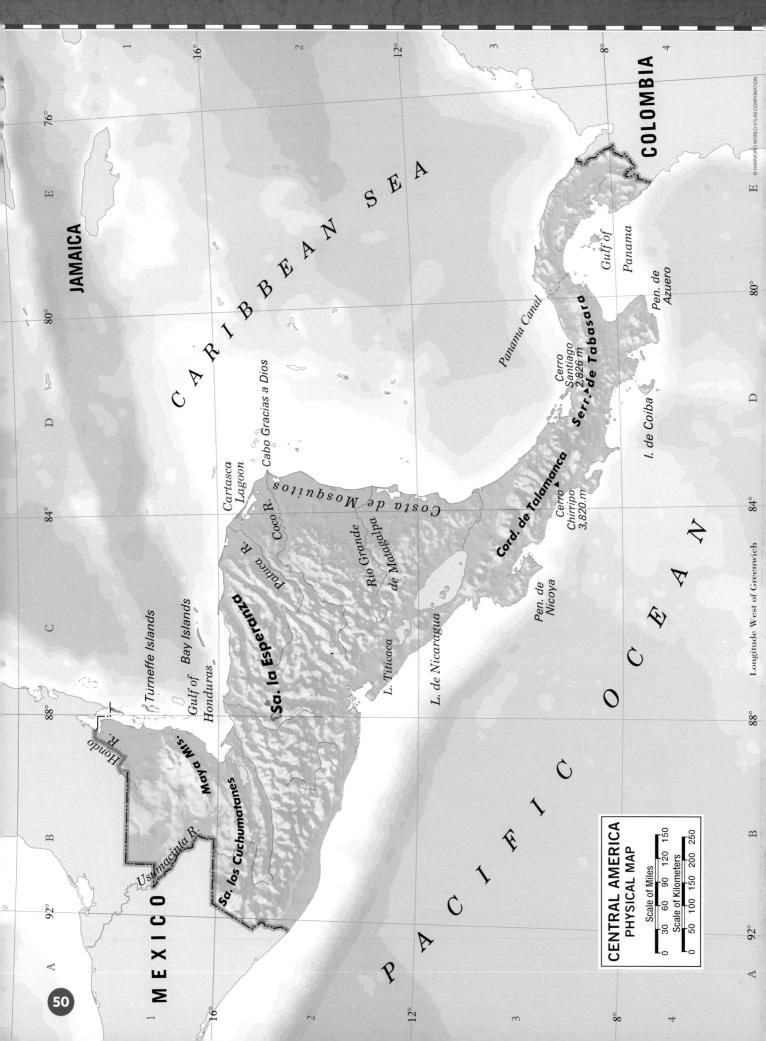

JAMAICA

CARIBBEAN SEA

MEXICO

Hondo R.

Maya Mts.

Usumacinta R.

Sa. los Cuchumatanes

Turneffe Islands

Gulf of Honduras

Bay Islands

Sa. la Esperanza

Patuca R.

Coco R.

Cartasca Lagoon

Cabo Gracias a Dios

Costa de Mosquitos

Rio Grande de Matagalpa

L. Titicaca

L. de Nicaragua

Pen. de Nicoya

Cord. de Talamanca

Cerro Chirripó 3,820 m

I. de Coiba

Panama Canal

Cerro Santiago 2,826 m

Serr. de Tabasara

Gulf of Panama

Pen. de Azuero

COLOMBIA

PACIFIC OCEAN

Longitude West of Greenwich

© HAMMOND WORLD ATLAS CORPORATION

CENTRAL AMERICA
PHYSICAL MAP

Scale of Miles

0   30   60   90   120   150

Scale of Kilometers

0   50   100   150   200   250

50

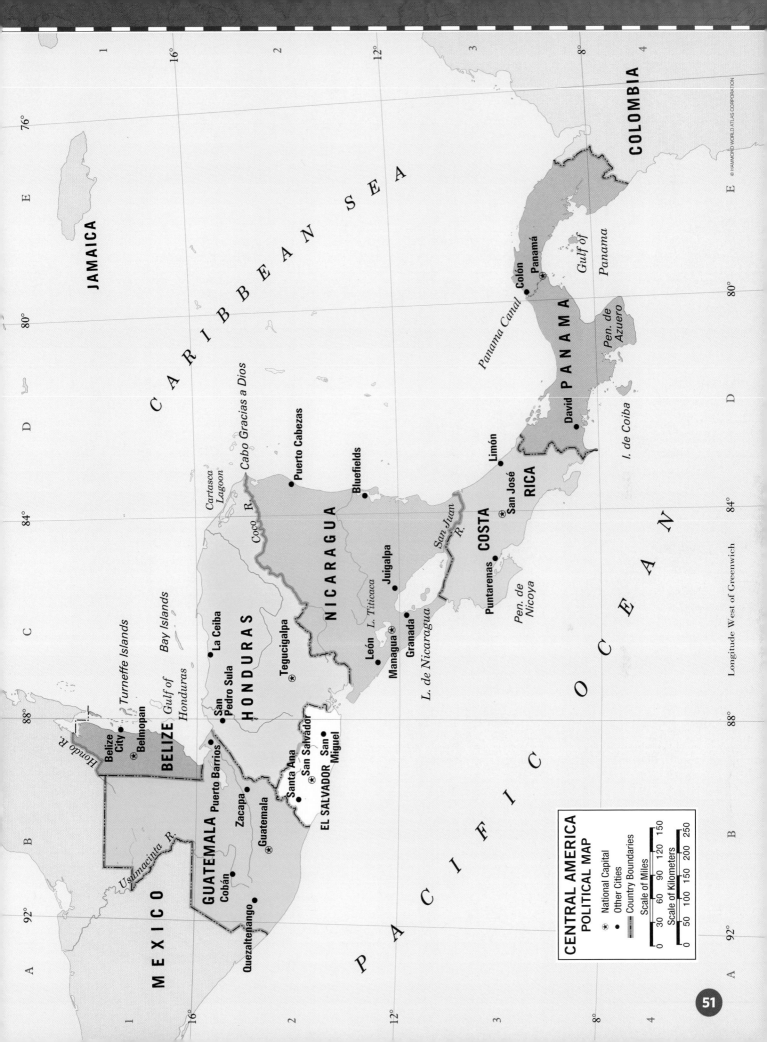

CENTRAL AMERICA
POLITICAL MAP

⊛ National Capital
● Other Cities
⋯⋯⋯ Country Boundaries

Scale of Miles
0 30 60 90 120 150

Scale of Kilometers
0 50 100 150 200 250

JAMAICA

COLOMBIA

CARIBBEAN SEA

PACIFIC OCEAN

MEXICO

BELIZE
Belize City
⊛ Belmopan
Turneffe Islands
Bay Islands
Gulf of Honduras
Hondo R.
Usumacinta R.

GUATEMALA
Puerto Barrios
Zacapa
⊛ Guatemala
Cobán
Quezaltenango
Santa Ana

EL SALVADOR
San Salvador ●
San Miguel ●

HONDURAS
La Ceiba
San Pedro Sula
⊛ Tegucigalpa

NICARAGUA
Puerto Cabezas
Bluefields
León
⊛ Managua
Granada
Juigalpa
L. Titicaca
L. de Nicaragua
Cartasca Lagoon
Cabo Gracias a Dios
Coco R.
San Juan R.

COSTA RICA
Limón
⊛ San José
Puntarenas
Pen. de Nicoya

PANAMA
Panamá
Colón
David
Panama Canal
Gulf of Panama
Pen. de Azuero
I. de Coiba

Longitude West of Greenwich

© HAMMOND WORLD ATLAS CORPORATION

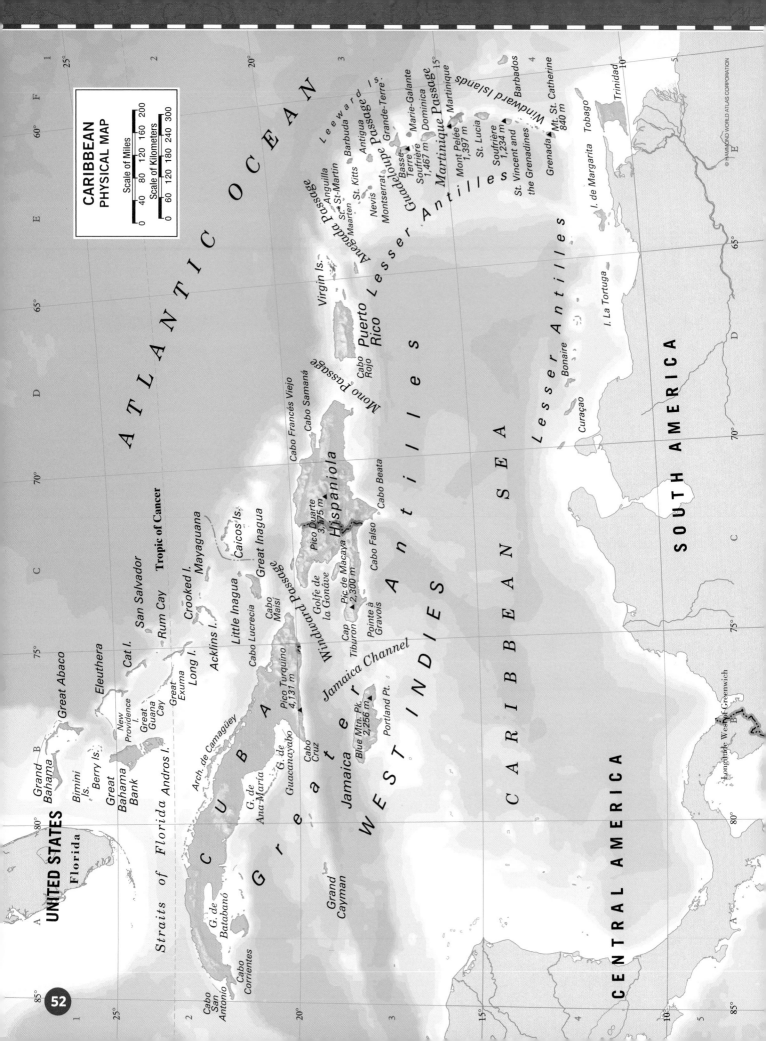

CARIBBEAN
PHYSICAL MAP

Scale of Miles
0 40 80 120 160 200

Scale of Kilometers
0 60 120 180 240 300

ATLANTIC OCEAN

UNITED STATES

Florida

Grand Bahama

Great Abaco

Bimini Is.

Berry Is.

Eleuthera

New Providence I.

Great Guana Cay

Great Bahama Bank

Cat I.

San Salvador

Rum Cay

Tropic of Cancer

Long I.

Great Exuma

Little Exuma

Crooked I.

Acklins I.

Mayaguana

Caicos Is.

Little Inagua

Great Inagua

Cabo Lucrecia

Cabo Maisi

Cabo Francés Viejo

Cabo Samaná

Mono Passage

Windward Passage

Straits of Florida

Andros I.

Arch. de Camagüey

G. de Ana-María

G. de Guacanayabo

G. de Batabanó

Cabo Corrientes

Cabo San Antonio

Cabo Cruz

C U B A

Pico Turquino 4,131 m

G r e a t e r

Jamaica

Grand Cayman

Blue Mtn. Pk. 2,256 m

Portland Pt.

Jamaica Channel

Cap Tiburon

Pointe à Gravois

Pic de Macaya 2,300 m

Cabo Falso

Golfe de la Gonâve

Pico Duarte 3,175 m

Hispaniola

Cabo Beata

A n t i l l e s

W E S T   I N D I E S

C A R I B B E A N   S E A

Virgin Is.

Puerto Rico

Cabo Rojo

Anegada Passage

Anguilla

St-Martin

St. Maarten

St. Kitts

Nevis

Montserrat

Barbuda

Antigua

Leeward Islands

Guadeloupe

Grande-Terre

Basse-Terre

Soufrière 1,467 m

Marie-Galante

Dominica

Martinique

Mont Pelée 1,397 m

Martinique Passage

St. Lucia

Soufrière 1,234 m

St. Vincent and the Grenadines

Windward Islands

Barbados

Mt. St. Catherine 840 m

Grenada

Tobago

Trinidad

L e s s e r   A n t i l l e s

L e s s e r   A n t i l l e s

I. de Margarita

I. La Tortuga

Bonaire

Curaçao

SOUTH AMERICA

CENTRAL AMERICA

Longitude West of Greenwich

© HAMMOND WORLD ATLAS CORPORATION

52

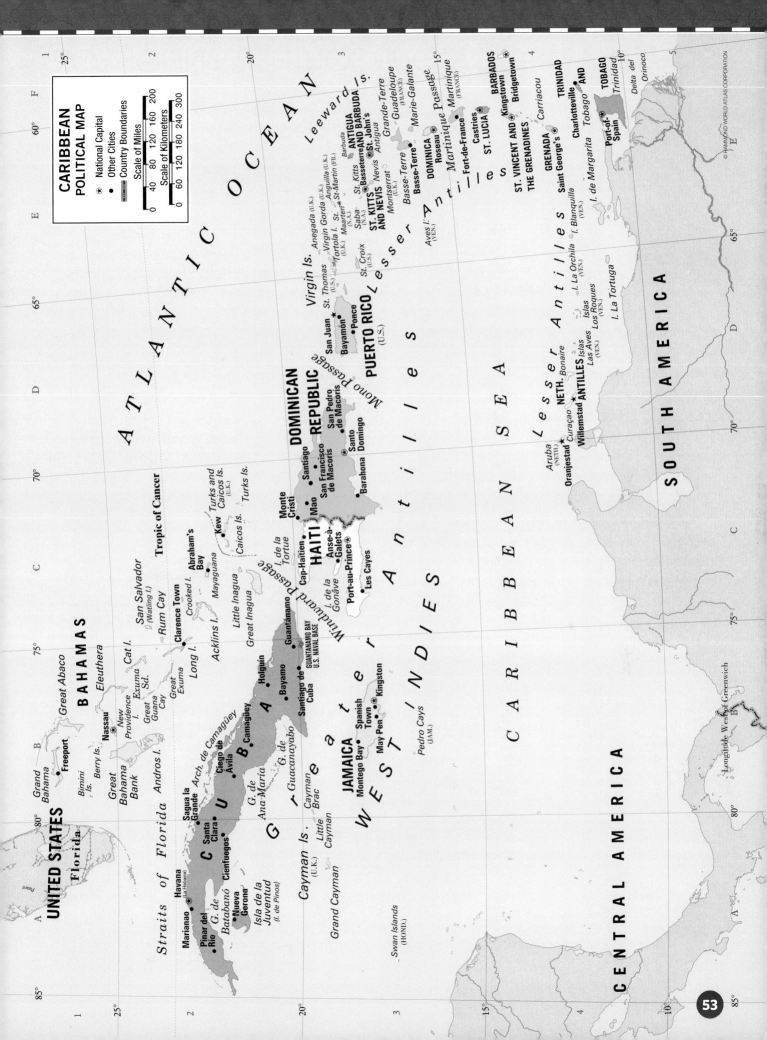

CARIBBEAN POLITICAL MAP

⊛ National Capital
• Other Cities
━━━ Country Boundaries

Scale of Miles
0 40 80 120 160 200

Scale of Kilometers
0 60 120 180 240 300

ATLANTIC OCEAN

UNITED STATES
Florida

BAHAMAS

Grand Bahama
Great Abaco
Freeport
Bimini Is.
Berry Is.
Nassau
New Providence
Eleuthera
Cat I.
San Salvador (Watling I.)
Rum Cay
Great Exuma
Exuma Sd.
Great Guana Cay
Long I.
Clarence Town
Crooked I.
Abraham's Bay
Acklins I.
Mayaguana
Little Inagua
Great Inagua
Kew
Turks and Caicos Is. (U.K.)
Caicos Is.
Turks Is.

Tropic of Cancer

Straits of Florida

Marianao
Havana (La Habana)
Pinar del Río
G. de Batabanó
Cienfuegos
Santa Clara
Sagua la Grande
Nueva Gerona
Isla de la Juventud (I. de Pinos)
Great Bahama Bank
Andros I.

C U B A
Ciego de Ávila
G. de Ana María
Arch. de Camagüey
Camagüey
Holguín
Bayamo
G. de Guacanayabo
Santiago de Cuba

Cayman Is. (U.K.)
Little Cayman
Cayman Brac
Grand Cayman

JAMAICA
Montego Bay
May Pen
Spanish Town
Kingston

Pedro Cays (JAM.)

Swan Islands (HOND.)

Greater Antilles

WEST INDIES

CARIBBEAN SEA

GUANTÁNAMO BAY
U.S. NAVAL BASE
Guantánamo

Monte Cristi
Mao
I. de la Tortue
Cap-Haïtien

HAITI
Anse-à-Galets
I. de la Gonâve
Port-au-Prince
Les Cayes

Windward Passage

DOMINICAN REPUBLIC
Santiago
San Francisco de Macorís
San Pedro de Macorís
Barahona
Santo Domingo

Mono Passage

PUERTO RICO (U.S.)
San Juan
Bayamón
Ponce

Virgin Is.

Lesser Antilles

Anegada (U.K.)
Virgin Gorda (U.K.)
St. Thomas (U.S.)
Tortola I. (U.K.)
St. Croix (U.S.)
Anguilla (U.K.)
St.-Martin (FR.)
Maarten (N.L.)
Saba (N.L.)
St. Eustatius (N.L.)
St. Kitts
Basseterre
ST. KITTS AND NEVIS
Nevis
Montserrat (U.K.)

Leeward Is.

Barbuda
ANTIGUA AND BARBUDA
St. John's
Antigua

Guadeloupe (FRANCE)
Grande-Terre
Basse-Terre
Marie-Galante

DOMINICA
Roseau

Martinique (FRANCE)
Fort-de-France

ST. LUCIA
Castries

Aves I. (VEN.)

ST. VINCENT AND THE GRENADINES
Kingstown

BARBADOS
Bridgetown

Carriacou

GRENADA
Saint George's

Lesser Antilles

I. de Margarita
I. Blanquilla (VEN.)
I. La Orchila (VEN.)
Las Aves Islas (VEN.)
Los Roques Islas (VEN.)
I. La Tortuga

TRINIDAD AND TOBAGO
TOBAGO
Trinidad
Charlotteville
TRINIDAD
Port-of-Spain

Aruba (NETH.)
Oranjestad
Curaçao
Willemstad
Bonaire
NETH. ANTILLES

Delta del Orinoco

SOUTH AMERICA

CENTRAL AMERICA

Longitude West of Greenwich

53

SOUTH AMERICA OUR SOUTHERN NEIGHBOR

Coffee

South America is the Earth's fourth-largest continent. In the north, it meets North America at the Isthmus of Panama. In the south, it is near the coldest continent, Antarctica. However, most of South America lies in the hot, tropic zone near the equator. It is bordered by the Atlantic and Pacific Oceans and the Caribbean Sea.

The equator crosses South America at the mouth of the Amazon River. The Amazon is the world's second-longest river and the one that carries the most water. In places, it is so wide a person cannot see across it.

The world's largest tropical rain forest, or selva, is found in the Amazon River Basin. This lowland region is always hot and wet. Trees grow so close together they form a tent-like roof, or canopy. Very little sunlight ever reaches the ground.

The Andes Mountains stretch like a backbone down the Pacific coast of South America. They are the longest and second-highest mountains on Earth. Many of the tallest peaks are volcanoes. Lake Titicaca, on a high plateau, is the Earth's highest navigable lake.

Large areas of South America have very few people. Much of the land is not easy to live on. In the north, the Llanos are hot, treeless plains. Dense forest covers the remote Guiana Highlands. In northern Chile, the Atacama Desert is one of the driest places on Earth. In the southeast, Patagonia is a dry, windswept region with poor soil.

Most South Americans live in just a few regions. The highlands of the northern Andes have a warm climate and long growing season. The Pampas are broad, fertile plains with a mild climate. Here, farmers grow wheat and corn, and ranchers raise sheep and cattle. The narrow coastal lowlands and nearby Brazilian Highlands have many people. Coffee and bananas are the main crops.

South America has twelve nations and one state. Brazil is by far the largest country. Its people speak Portuguese. Spanish is the language in Venezuela, Colombia, Ecuador, Peru, Bolivia, Chile, Argentina, Paraguay and Uruguay. In Guyana, English is spoken. Dutch is the language of Suriname. French Guiana is a department, or state, of France.

The Incas were one of the first people of South America. Over 450 years ago, they were conquered by Spanish soldiers from Europe. Today, most South Americans have European, African or Native American heritage. Many are mestizos, which means part Indian and part European.

CONTINENT CLOSEUP

- Brazil grows more oranges and coffee than any other nation on Earth.

- The world's second highest standard gauge railroad is in Peru. It climbs the Andes to over three miles above sea level.

- Large water mammals called manatees, or sea cows, live in the Amazon River, often growing to over 1,000 pounds.

- La Paz, one of Bolivia's two capitals, is over two miles above sea level.

▼ There are many rich mineral deposits in South America. This open-pit copper mine is in Chile. Find out what copper is used for.

CITIES WITH OVER 1,000,000
INHABITANTS

POPULATION DISTRIBUTION

DENSITY PER		SQ. MI.	SQ. KM.	SQ. MI.	SQ. KM.
SQ. MI.	SQ. KM.	130 to 260	50 to 100	3 to 25	1 to 10
OVER 260	OVER 100	25 to 130	10 to 50	UNDER 3	UNDER 1

LAND USE

- CEREALS, LIVESTOCK
- LIVESTOCK & MIXED FARMING
- TRUCK FARMING, SPECIAL CROPS
- DIVERSIFIED TROPICAL CROPS
- LIVESTOCK GRAZING & RANCHING
- FORESTS
- NONPRODUCTIVE

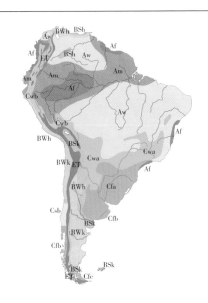

CLIMATE

HUMID TROPICAL
- Af   NO DRY SEASON
- Am   SHORT DRY SEASON
- Aw   DRY WINTER

DRY
- BS   SEMIARID   ⎤ h HOT
- BW   ARID   ⎦ k COLD

HUMID WARM
- Cf   NO DRY SEASON
- Cw   DRY WINTER
- Cs   DRY SUMMER

COLD POLAR
- ET   SHORT COOL SUMMER, LONG COLD WINTER

a   HOT SUMMER
b   COOL SUMMER
c   SHORT COOL SUMMER

AFTER KOEPPEN-GEIGER

VEGETATION

TROPICAL FOREST
- TROPICAL RAINFOREST
- LIGHT TROPICAL FOREST
- WOODLAND AND SHRUB

TROPICAL GRASSLAND
- GRASS AND SHRUB (SAVANNA)
- WOODED SAVANNA

MID-LATITUDE FOREST
- NEEDLELEAF FOREST
- MIXED NEEDLELEAF AND BROADLEAF FOREST
- WOODLAND AND SHRUB (MEDITERRANEAN)

MID-LATITUDE GRASSLAND
- SHORT GRASS (STEPPE)
- TALL GRASS (PRAIRIE) AND WOODED STEPPE

- DESERT AND DESERT SHRUB
- TUNDRA AND ALPINE
- UNCLASSIFIED HIGHLANDS

▼ Rio de Janiero is Brazil's second largest city. It is a famous tourist destination in South America.

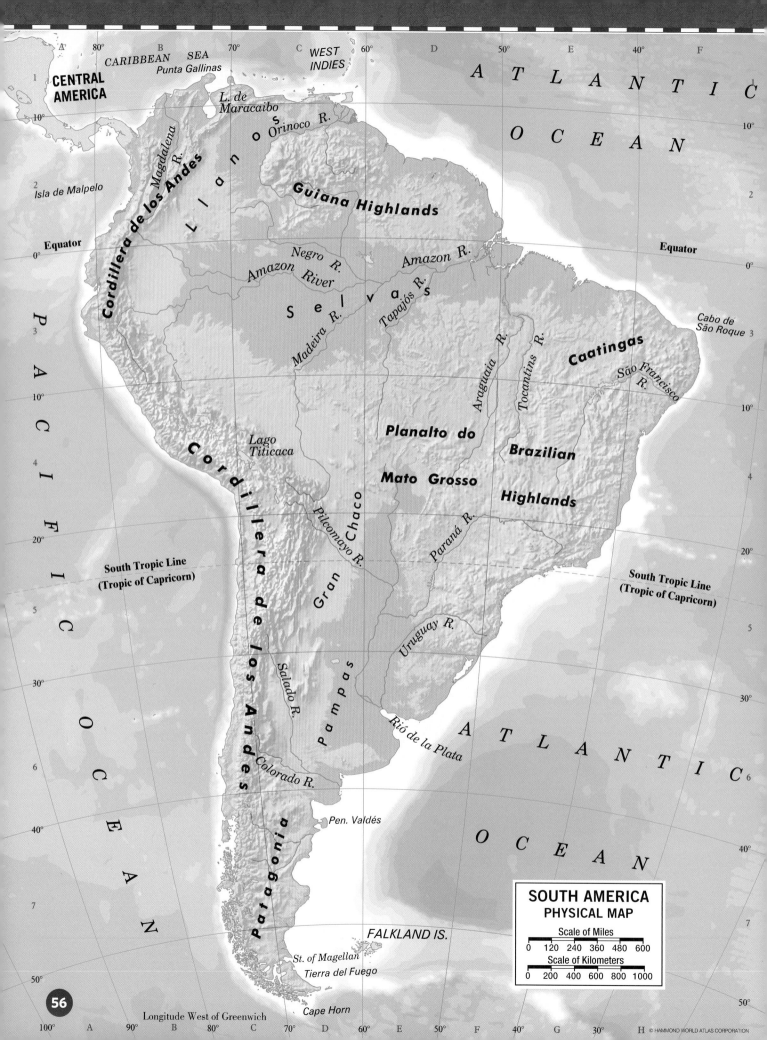

CENTRAL
AMERICA

CARIBBEAN SEA
Punta Gallinas

WEST
INDIES

ATLANTIC

OCEAN

Isla de Malpelo

L. de
Maracaibo

Orinoco R.

Llanos

Cordillera de los Andes

Magdalena R.

Guiana Highlands

Equator
0°

Negro R.

Amazon River

Amazon R.

Selvas

Madeira R.

Tapajós R.

Cabo de
São Roque

Araguaia R.

Tocantins R.

Caatingas

São Francisco R.

Planalto do

Mato Grosso

Brazilian

Highlands

Lago
Titicaca

Cordillera de los Andes

Pilcomayo R.

Gran Chaco

Paraná R.

South Tropic Line
(Tropic of Capricorn)

South Tropic Line
(Tropic of Capricorn)

Uruguay R.

PACIFIC

Salado R.

Pampas

Rió de la Plata

ATLANTIC

Colorado R.

OCEAN

Patagonia

Pen. Valdés

OCEAN

OCEAN

SOUTH AMERICA
PHYSICAL MAP

Scale of Miles

| 0 | 120 | 240 | 360 | 480 | 600 |

Scale of Kilometers

| 0 | 200 | 400 | 600 | 800 | 1000 |

FALKLAND IS.

St. of Magellan
Tierra del Fuego

Cape Horn

Longitude West of Greenwich

© HAMMOND WORLD ATLAS CORPORATION

SOUTH AMERICA
POLITICAL MAP

⊛ National Capital
● Other Cities
▬▬ Country Boundaries

Scale of Miles

0 120 240 360 480 600

Scale of Kilometers

0 200 400 600 800 1000

CARIBBEAN SEA

Punta Gallinas

WEST INDIES

CENTRAL AMERICA

Barranquilla

Maracaibo

Caracas

L. de Maracaibo

Orinoco R.

VENEZUELA

Medellín

Quibdó

Bogotá

Cali

Isla de Malpelo

COLUMBIA

GUYANA

Georgetown

Paramaribo

FRENCH GUIANA

SURINAME

Cayenne

Guiana Highlands

Equator

Quito

ECUADOR

Guayaquil

Negro R.

Amazon R.

Manaus

Amazon R.

Belém

Fortaleza

Cabo de São Roque

Amazon River

Madeira R.

Tapajós R.

B R A Z I L

Chiclayo

P E R U

Callao

Lima

Cusco

Lago Titicaca

La Paz

Arequipa

Arica

BOLIVIA

Sucre

Araguaia River

Tocantins R.

São Francisco R.

Recife

Salvador

Brasília

Belo Horizonte

Pilcomayo R.

PARAGUAY

Paraná R.

South Tropic Line (Tropic of Capricorn)

Antofagasta

La Quiaca

San Miguel de Tucumán

Asunción

Santiago del Estero

Córdoba

A R G E N T I N A

Santa Fe

Rosario

Salado R.

Uruguay R.

São Paulo

Santos

Curitiba

Rio de Janeiro

South Tropic Line (Tropic of Capricorn)

Valparaíso

Santiago

Concepción

Buenos Aires

La Plata

URUGUAY

Montevideo

Río de la Plata

C H I L E

Cordillera de los Andes

Pen. Valdés

FALKLAND IS.

Punta Arenas

St. of Magellan

Tierra del Fuego

Longitude West of Greenwich

Cape Horn

PACIFIC OCEAN

ATLANTIC OCEAN

57

© HAMMOND WORLD ATLAS CORPORATION

AFRICA THE HOTTEST CONTINENT

Lion

Africa is the second-largest continent. It is bordered by the Atlantic and Indian Oceans and by the Mediterranean and Red Seas. In the northeast, Africa joins Asia at the Sinai Peninsula.

Africa is the hottest continent on Earth. The equator passes through the middle of the continent. Most of Africa lies in the tropic zone. Except in the highlands, the weather is hot all year. Once it was 136° in Libya, the highest temperature ever recorded on Earth.

Look at the physical map on page 60. The Sahara is the world's largest desert. It extends from the Atlantic Ocean to the Red Sea. At the equator, Africa is covered by a hot, wet rain forest. North and south of the equator, most of Africa is dry grassland or desert. Only the northwest and southern tips of the continent have mild climates.

Earth's longest river, the Nile, flows north from Lake Victoria to the Mediterranean Sea. At the mouth of the Nile is a wide, fertile delta. Good soil is also found along its banks over its entire course. In fact, the Nile River Valley is the world's largest oasis, a place in the desert with water and fertile soil.

Look at the population map on page 59. You can see that many people live along the Nile. The civilization of ancient Egypt centered around this great river.

Though Africa has long rivers, it lacks natural harbors along the coasts. Waterfalls and rapids prevent ships from sailing inland. Even so, most Africans live near rivers, lakes and coasts. The Niger and Congo Rivers are two other important waterways.

Most of Africa is a low plateau. Africa's highlands are in the east along the Great Rift Valley. This region of large, deep lakes runs from the Red Sea to the Zambezi River. Animals such as giraffes, elephants, lions and zebras can be seen here.

There are more than fifty independent nations in Africa. Sudan is the largest and Nigeria has the most people. Africa's Arabs live in the north. Black Africans of many different ethnic groups live south of the Sahara. Each group has its own language, beliefs and customs. In fact, more than 800 languages are spoken in Africa.

Most Africans are farmers who live in small villages. Others herd cattle. Africans grow crops for their own use and for sale. Major exports include coffee, cocoa beans and cotton. Although little manufacturing is done in Africa, the continent has a wealth of resources, including gold, diamonds, copper and oil.

CONTINENT CLOSEUP

- Ships sail inland over a thousand miles up the Congo River.
- The first human heart transplant took place in South Africa in 1967.
- Millions of wild animals live on the Serengeti plain in Tanzania. They are protected from hunters.
- Seventeen African nations became independent in 1960.

▼ The Pyramids in Egypt are more than four thousand years old.

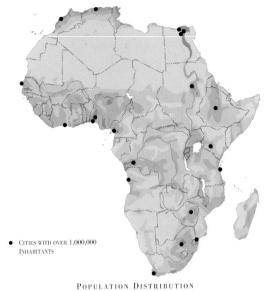

POPULATION DISTRIBUTION

- ● CITIES WITH OVER 1,000,000 INHABITANTS

DENSITY PER					
SQ. MI.	SQ. KM.	130 TO 260 / 50 TO 100		3 TO 25 / 1 TO 10	
OVER 260	OVER 100	25 TO 130 / 10 TO 50		UNDER 3 / UNDER 1	

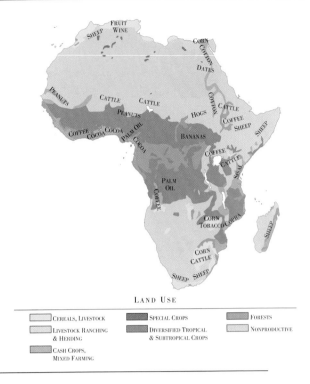

LAND USE

CEREALS, LIVESTOCK	SPECIAL CROPS	FORESTS
LIVESTOCK RANCHING & HERDING	DIVERSIFIED TROPICAL & SUBTROPICAL CROPS	NONPRODUCTIVE
CASH CROPS, MIXED FARMING		

CLIMATE

HUMID TROPICAL
- Af NO DRY SEASON
- Am SHORT DRY SEASON
- Aw DRY WINTER

DRY
- BS SEMIARID
- BW ARID
  - h HOT
  - k COLD

HUMID WARM
- Cf NO DRY SEASON
- Cw DRY WINTER
- Cs DRY SUMMER
- a HOT SUMMER
- b COOL SUMMER

AFTER KOEPPEN-GEIGER

VEGETATION

TROPICAL FOREST
- TROPICAL RAINFOREST
- LIGHT TROPICAL FOREST
- WOODLAND AND SHRUB

TROPICAL GRASSLAND
- GRASS AND SHRUB (SAVANNA)
- WOODED SAVANNA

MID-LATITUDE FOREST
- MIXED NEEDLELEAF AND BROADLEAF FOREST
- WOODLAND AND SHRUB (MEDITERRANEAN)

MID-LATITUDE GRASSLAND
- SHORT GRASS (STEPPE)

- DESERT AND DESERT SHRUB
- RIVER VALLEY AND OASIS
- UNCLASSIFIED HIGHLANDS

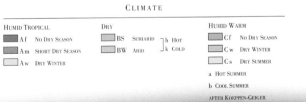

▼ The port city of Alexandria, Egypt is on the Mediterranean Sea.

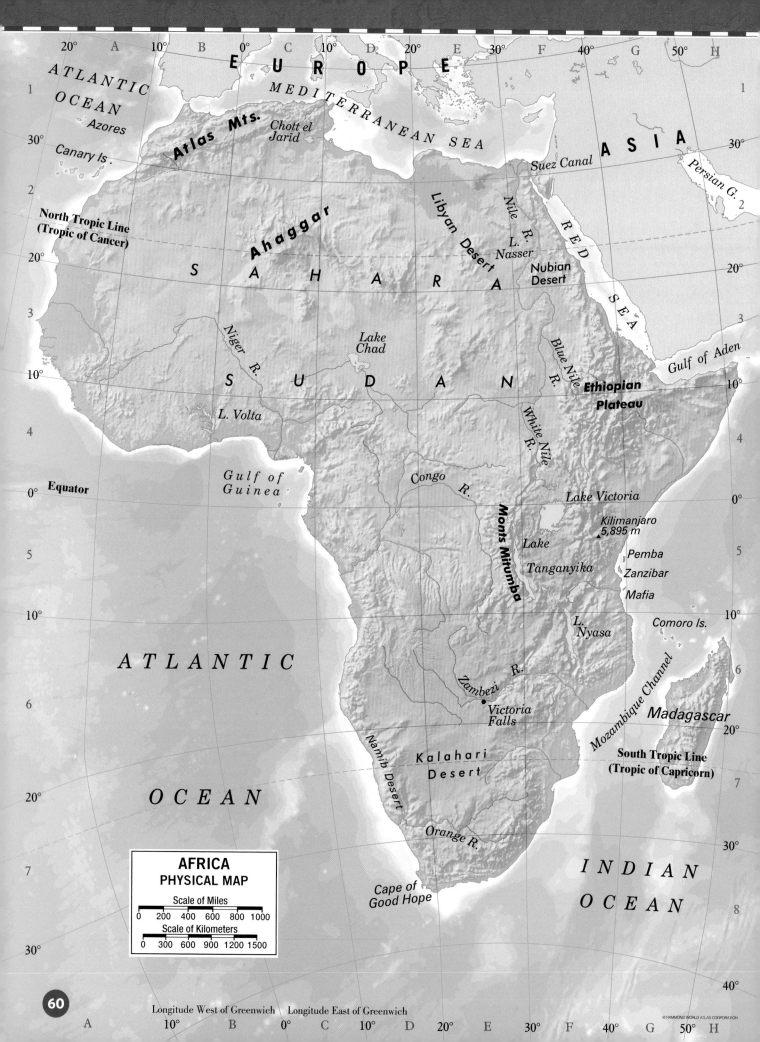

AFRICA
PHYSICAL MAP

Scale of Miles
0 200 400 600 800 1000

Scale of Kilometers
0 300 600 900 1200 1500

ATLANTIC OCEAN
Azores
Canary Is.
North Tropic Line (Tropic of Cancer)
Equator
ATLANTIC OCEAN

EUROPE
MEDITERRANEAN SEA
Atlas Mts.
Chott el Jarid
Suez Canal
ASIA
Persian G.

SAHARA
Ahaggar
Libyan Desert
Nile R.
L. Nasser
RED SEA
Nubian Desert
Gulf of Aden

Niger R.
Lake Chad
SUDAN
Blue Nile R.
Ethiopian Plateau
L. Volta
Gulf of Guinea
Congo R.
White Nile R.
Lake Victoria
Kilimanjaro 5,895 m
Pemba
Zanzibar
Mafia
Monts Mitumba
Lake Tanganyika
L. Nyasa
Comoro Is.

Zambezi R.
Victoria Falls
Mozambique Channel
Madagascar
South Tropic Line (Tropic of Capricorn)

Namib Desert
Kalahari Desert
Orange R.
Cape of Good Hope
INDIAN OCEAN

60

Longitude West of Greenwich   Longitude East of Greenwich

© HAMMOND WORLD ATLAS CORPORATION

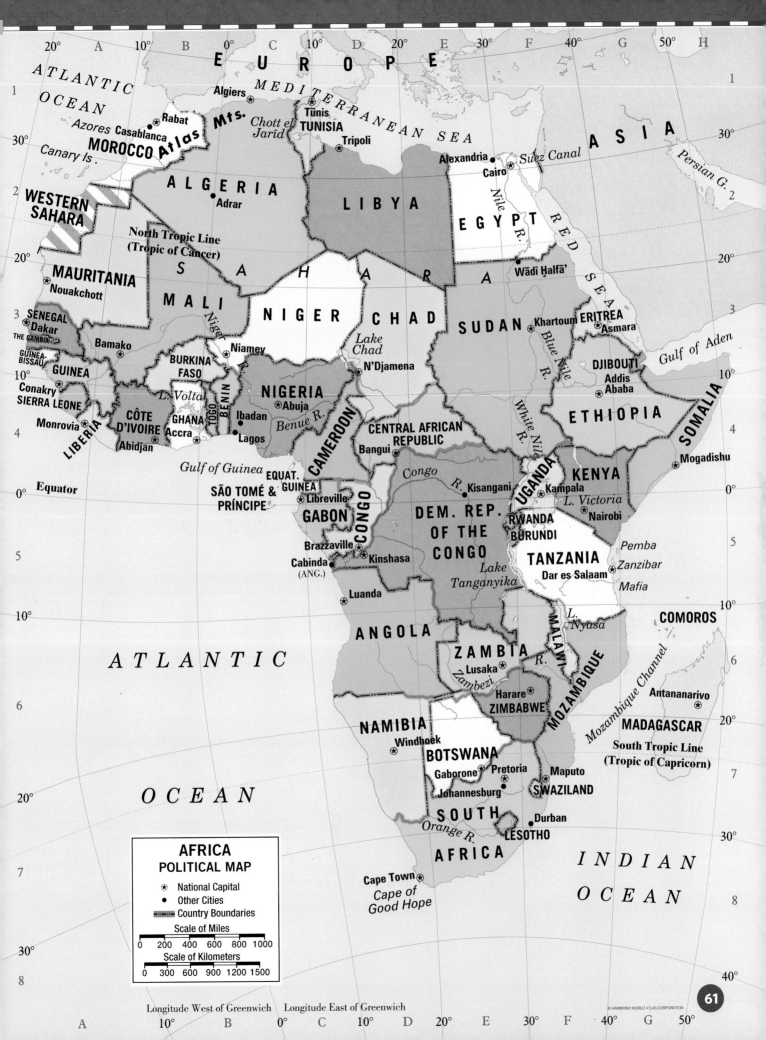

AFRICA
POLITICAL MAP

⊛ National Capital
• Other Cities
━━━ Country Boundaries

Scale of Miles

0 200 400 600 800 1000

Scale of Kilometers

0 300 600 900 1200 1500

EUROPE

ASIA

ATLANTIC OCEAN

MEDITERRANEAN SEA

Algiers

Rabat
Azores Casablanca
MOROCCO Atlas Mts.
Canary Is.

Tūnis
TUNISIA
Tripoli

Chott el Jarīd

ALGERIA

Adrar

LIBYA

Alexandria
Cairo Suez Canal

EGYPT

Nile R.

Persian G.

RED SEA

WESTERN SAHARA

North Tropic Line
(Tropic of Cancer)

MAURITANIA
Nouakchott

S A H A R A

Wādī Ḥalfā'

SENEGAL
Dakar
THE GAMBIA
GUINEA-BISSAU
GUINEA
Conakry
SIERRA LEONE
Monrovia
LIBERIA

MALI

Bamako

Niger R.

NIGER

N'Djamena

CHAD

Lake Chad

SUDAN

Khartoum
Blue Nile R.

ERITREA
Asmara

DJIBOUTI
Addis Ababa

Gulf of Aden

BURKINA FASO

Niamey

L. Volta

CÔTE D'IVOIRE
GHANA
Accra
Abidjan

TOGO
BENIN
Ibadan
Lagos

NIGERIA
Abuja

Benue R.

CAMEROON

CENTRAL AFRICAN REPUBLIC

Bangui

White Nile R.

ETHIOPIA

SOMALIA

Mogadishu

Gulf of Guinea

SÃO TOMÉ & PRÍNCIPE

EQUAT. GUINEA

Libreville

GABON

CONGO

Brazzaville
Cabinda
(ANG.)
Kinshasa

Congo R.
Kisangani

DEM. REP. OF THE CONGO

UGANDA
Kampala

RWANDA
BURUNDI

L. Victoria
Nairobi

KENYA

Equator

Luanda

Lake Tanganyika

TANZANIA
Dar es Salaam

Pemba
Zanzibar
Mafia

ATLANTIC OCEAN

ANGOLA

L. Nyasa

COMOROS

ZAMBIA
Lusaka

MALAWI

Zambezi R.

Harare
ZIMBABWE

MOZAMBIQUE

Mozambique Channel

Antananarivo

MADAGASCAR

South Tropic Line
(Tropic of Capricorn)

NAMIBIA
Windhoek

BOTSWANA
Gaborone
Pretoria
Johannesburg

Maputo
SWAZILAND

Orange R.

SOUTH AFRICA

LESOTHO

Durban

Cape Town
Cape of Good Hope

INDIAN OCEAN

© HAMMOND WORLD ATLAS CORPORATION

Longitude West of Greenwich Longitude East of Greenwich

EUROPE THE MOST CROWDED CONTINENT

Olives

Europe is the second-smallest continent. It stretches north to the cold Arctic Ocean and south to the warm Mediterranean Sea. The Atlantic Ocean borders Europe on the west. On the east, Europe meets Asia at the Ural Mountains and Caspian Sea. Since Europe and Asia are part of the same great expanse of land, some people think of them as one gigantic continent, **Eurasia**.

Europe may be thought of as a huge peninsula of Eurasia. It is broken into many smaller peninsulas. Look at the physical map on page 64. Find the Scandinavian Peninsula in the north and the Iberian and Balkan Peninsulas in the south.

On three sides, Europe's land is cut by seas, gulfs and bays. Most of Europe is close to a seacoast. Inland, great rivers, such as the Volga, Danube and Rhine, provide waterways. It is not surprising that Europeans became sailors and explorers. During the Age of Exploration, many European nations spread their languages and culture to the Americas.

Many of the continent's countries are isolated by rugged mountains. The Alps run from southern France across the center of Europe to Slovenia. They separate Italy from its neighbors. The Pyrenees form a natural border between Spain and France. The Balkans and Carpathians also separate many small nations. Compare the physical and political maps of Europe to see which ones.

Most of Europe has a mild climate, even though it lies closer to the North Pole than to the equator. Warm breezes reach as far north as Norway. These winds are heated by the Gulf Stream, a warm current of the Atlantic Ocean.

Europe is the most crowded continent. Look at the population map on page 63. Notice the very crowded lands that extend across the middle of the continent. Much of this strip is the fertile European Plain, a low region of excellent farmland. The leading products map shows that potatoes, sugar beets and grain crops are grown here.

Iron ore and coal are also plentiful. Together, they are used to make steel. Europe is very highly developed, with manufacturing centers throughout. In fact, this is where the Industrial Revolution began!

Europe has over forty nations. Russia is the largest country in the world. It extends from Europe across Asia to the Pacific Ocean. Tiny Vatican City, the smallest nation, is the size of a few city blocks.

CONTINENT CLOSEUP

- Millions of people in the Netherlands live on land taken from the sea.

- Italy is the world's largest grower of grapes and artichokes. Over half of the world's olives come from Italy and Spain.

- London had the first subway, in 1863, but Moscow has the world's second busiest, carrying more than six million people a day.

- Switzerland, surrounded by the Alps, has not been at war since 1515.

Netherlands is famous for tulips and windmills. ▶

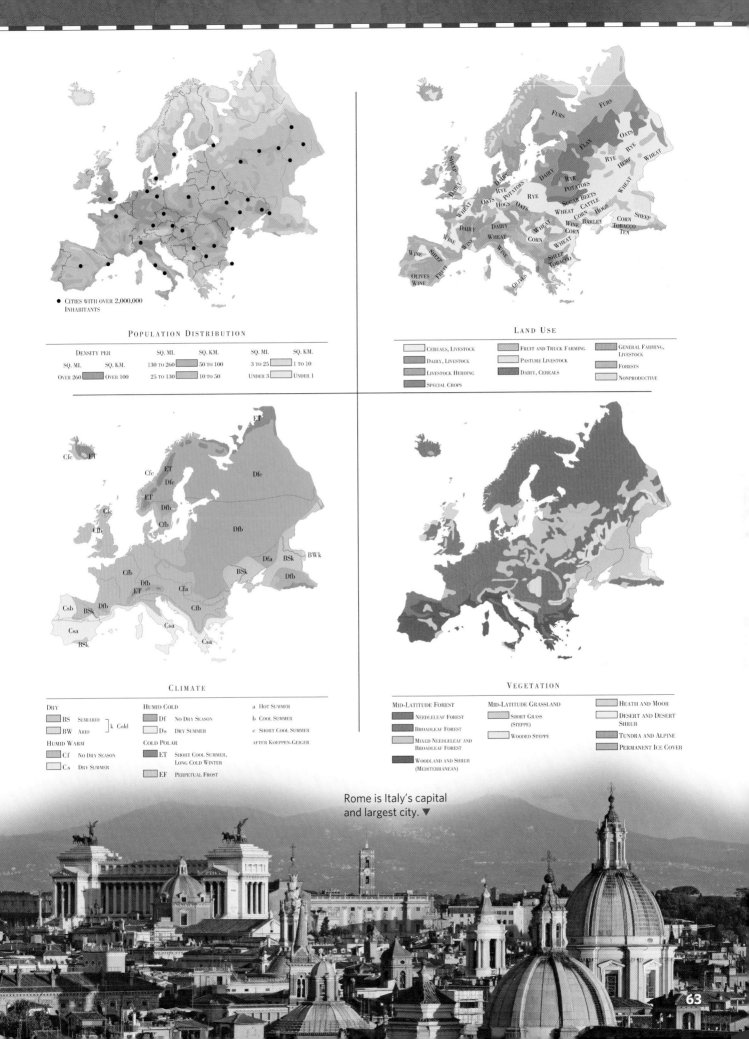

POPULATION DISTRIBUTION

● CITIES WITH OVER 2,000,000 INHABITANTS

DENSITY PER							
SQ. MI.	SQ. KM.	SQ. MI.	SQ. KM.	SQ. MI.	SQ. KM.	SQ. MI.	SQ. KM.
OVER 260	OVER 100	130 TO 260	50 TO 100	25 TO 130	10 TO 50	3 TO 25	1 TO 10
						UNDER 3	UNDER 1

LAND USE

CEREALS, LIVESTOCK	FRUIT AND TRUCK FARMING	GENERAL FARMING, LIVESTOCK
DAIRY, LIVESTOCK	PASTURE LIVESTOCK	FORESTS
LIVESTOCK HERDING	DAIRY, CEREALS	NONPRODUCTIVE
SPECIAL CROPS		

CLIMATE

AFTER KOEPPEN-GEIGER

DRY
- BS SEMIARID] k Cold
- BW ARID]

HUMID WARM
- Cf NO DRY SEASON
- Cs DRY SUMMER

HUMID COLD
- Df NO DRY SEASON
- Ds DRY SUMMER

a HOT SUMMER
b COOL SUMMER
c SHORT COOL SUMMER

COLD POLAR
- ET SHORT COOL SUMMER, LONG COLD WINTER
- EF PERPETUAL FROST

VEGETATION

MID-LATITUDE FOREST
- NEEDLELEAF FOREST
- BROADLEAF FOREST
- MIXED NEEDLELEAF AND BROADLEAF FOREST
- WOODLAND AND SHRUB (MEDITERRANEAN)

MID-LATITUDE GRASSLAND
- SHORT GRASS (STEPPE)
- WOODED STEPPE

- HEATH AND MOOR
- DESERT AND DESERT SHRUB
- TUNDRA AND ALPINE
- PERMANENT ICE COVER

Rome is Italy's capital and largest city. ▼

EUROPE
PHYSICAL MAP

Scale of Miles
0 180 360 540 620 900

Scale of Kilometers
0 300 600 900 1200 1500

Ural Mountains

Zhayyq R.
(Ural R.)

Caucasus

Aras R.

Volga R.

Volga Uplands

A S I A

Don R.

Don R.

Central Russian Uplands

Don R.

Dnipro R.

Black Sea

Crimea

Lake Onega

Lake Ladoga

Volga

R.

Arctic Circle

BARENTS SEA

Daugava R.

Dnister R.

Carpathian Mts.

Danube R.

Balkan Pen.

Aegean Sea

Crete

North European Plain

Oder R.

R.

Sava R.

Adriatic Sea

Apennines

Mt. Etna
3,323 m

Malta

MEDITERRANEAN SEA

Kjølen

Scandinavian Peninsula

Gulf of Bothnia

Baltic Sea

Elbe R.

Danube R.

Po R.

A L P S

Corsica

Sardinia

NORWEGIAN SEA

Rhine R.

Mont Blanc
4,807 m

Cyprus

NORTH SEA

Seine R.

BRITISH

Great Britain

ISLES

Thames

Loire R.

Pyrenees

Ebro R.

Iceland

Arctic Circle

Ireland

English Channel

Bay of Biscay

Duero R.

Tagus R.

Iberian Peninsula

Strait of Gibraltar

Gibraltar

A F R I C A

A T L A N T I C   O C E A N

Longitude West of Greenwich 0° Longitude East of Greenwich

© HAMMOND WORLD ATLAS CORPORATION

64

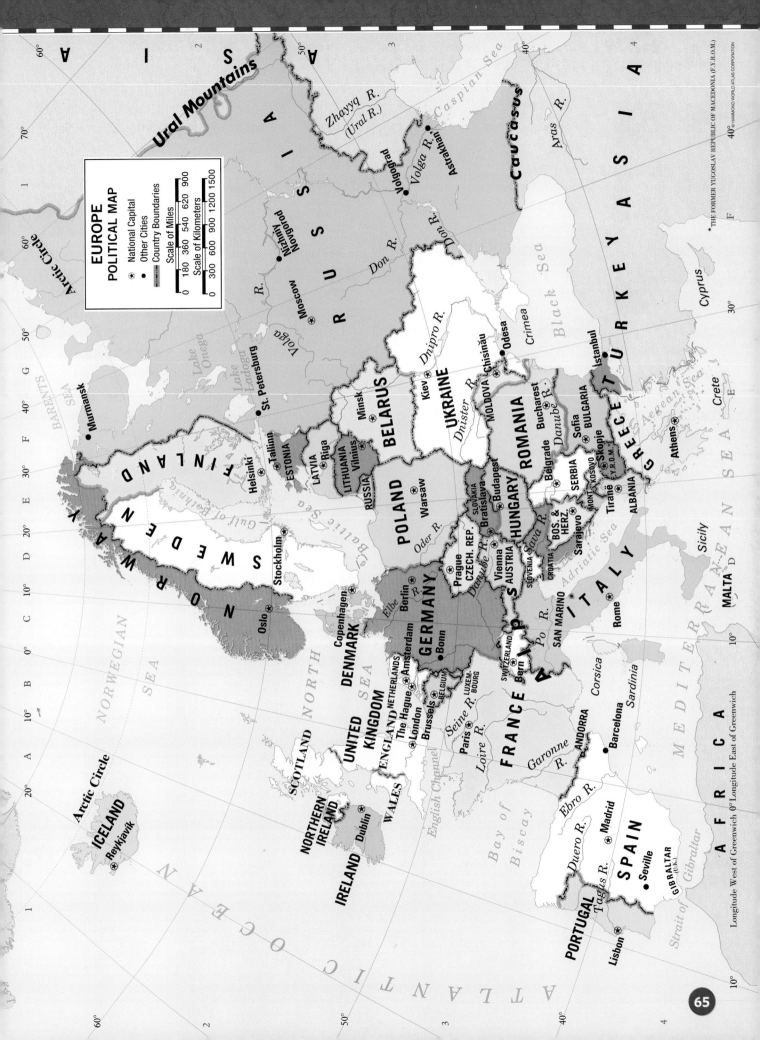

EUROPE
POLITICAL MAP

✪ National Capital
• Other Cities
Country Boundaries

Scale of Miles
0 180 360 540 620 900

Scale of Kilometers
0 300 600 900 1200 1500

ASIA

Ural Mountains

Zhayyq R. (Ural R.)

Caspian Sea

Caucasus

Aras R.

Volga R.

Astrakhan

Volgograd

Nizhniy Novgorod

Don R.

R.

Moscow

Volga

RUSSIA

Lake Onega

Lake Ladoga

St. Petersburg

Don R.

Dnipro R.

Odesa

Crimea

Black Sea

Kiev

UKRAINE

Dnister R.

MOLDOVA
Chisinău

Istanbul

TURKEY

Cyprus

Murmansk

BARENTS SEA

Arctic Circle

Helsinki

Tallinn

ESTONIA

Riga

LATVIA

LITHUANIA
Vilnius

Minsk

BELARUS

RUSSIA

POLAND

Warsaw

Oder R.

Bucharest

Danube R.

Sofia

BULGARIA

ROMANIA

Belgrade

SERBIA

Skopje
F.Y.R.O.M.

MONT.
KOSOVO

GREECE

Aegean Sea

Athens

Crete

Sicily

FINLAND

Gulf of Bothnia

Baltic Sea

SWEDEN

Stockholm

NORWAY

Oslo

Copenhagen

DENMARK

Berlin

Elbe R.

GERMANY

Bonn

Prague
CZECH. REP.

Danube R.

Vienna

AUSTRIA

SLOVAKIA
Bratislava

Budapest

HUNGARY

SLOVENIA
Sava R.

CROATIA

BOS. & HERZ.

Sarajevo

Tiranë

ALBANIA

Adriatic Sea

ITALY

Rome

SAN MARINO

Po R.

SWITZERLAND

Bern

SCOTLAND

NORTH SEA

UNITED KINGDOM

ENGLAND

WALES

NORTHERN IRELAND

IRELAND

Dublin

Amsterdam

The Hague

NETHERLANDS

London

Brussels

BELGIUM

LUXEM-BOURG

Paris

Seine R.

Loire R.

FRANCE

English Channel

Bay of Biscay

Garonne R.

ANDORRA

Barcelona

Ebro R.

Corsica

Sardinia

MALTA

M E D I T E R R A N E A N   S E A

ICELAND

Reykjavik

Arctic Circle

ATLANTIC OCEAN

NORWEGIAN SEA

PORTUGAL

Lisbon

Tagus R.

Duero R.

Madrid

SPAIN

Seville

GIBRALTAR (U.K.)

Strait of Gibraltar

AFRICA

Duero R.

*THE FORMER YUGOSLAV REPUBLIC OF MACEDONIA (F.Y.R.O.M.)

©HAMMOND WORLD ATLAS CORPORATION

Longitude West of Greenwich 0° Longitude East of Greenwich

65

ASIA THE LARGEST CONTINENT

Panda Bears

Asia ranks first in the world in many ways. It has more land and more people than any other continent. Earth's highest mountains, lowest land and deepest lake are here. Most of the largest nation, Russia, is in Asia. The two nations with the most people, China and India, are here.

Asia extends from frozen wastes at the Arctic Ocean to blistering deserts in the central and southwestern regions. Much of the continent's land cannot support more than a few people because of the harsh climate.

Asia's coasts are carved into peninsulas. In the southwest, the Arabian Peninsula is the largest on Earth. Most of India is a peninsula, as is Indochina in the southeast.

Hundreds of islands, some small, some very large, form a chain at the edge of the Pacific Ocean, from the far north to south of the equator. Japan, the Philippines and Indonesia are among the nations that are found on these islands. Other smaller islands are also found in the Indian Ocean.

The Himalayas, between China and India, are the world's highest mountain system. Here is Mount Everest, the highest point on Earth. North of these mountains is the plateau of Tibet, the largest and highest plateau on Earth.

Asia can be divided into six land regions. **Southwest Asia** extends from the Black Sea to the Arabian Sea. It is an area of large deserts and rich supplies of oil. India lies in **South Asia**, while Japan and China are in **East Asia**. These two regions are crossed by great rivers, have fertile farmland and mild climates. They are among the most densely populated places on Earth.

Southeast Asia includes the Indochina Peninsula and the islands nearby. This region is covered by tropical rain forests. It has a hot climate year round. In contrast, **North Asia** includes the plain of Siberia, the coldest inhabited area on Earth. **Central Asia** includes Mongolia and western China. Little rain falls in this area of high mountains, plateaus and deserts.

Asia has long been famous for its spices, tea and cotton. Rice and wheat are the most important food crops. Russia, China, Japan and South Korea manufacture many goods. Asia has many large, crowded cities such as Tokyo, Shanghai, Calcutta and Seoul. Even so, most Asians still grow their own food and live in small, rural villages.

The world's earliest civilizations arose in Asia. All of the world's major religions began here. From Israel to India, from Saudi Arabia to Japan, Asians are as varied as their vast continent.

CONTINENT CLOSEUP

- The Great Wall of China is more than 4,000 miles long.

- Lake Baykal, Russia, the deepest lake in the world, is over a mile deep in many parts.

- Mount Everest, the world's highest peak, was first climbed in 1953 by Sir Edmund Hillary and Tenzing Norgay.

- More than half the world's known oil reserves are found in Southwest Asia.

Some areas of Asia have fertile soils. In these places farming is very important. These farmers are growing rice–Asia's chief food crop. Most farms are small. Most work is done by hand. ▼

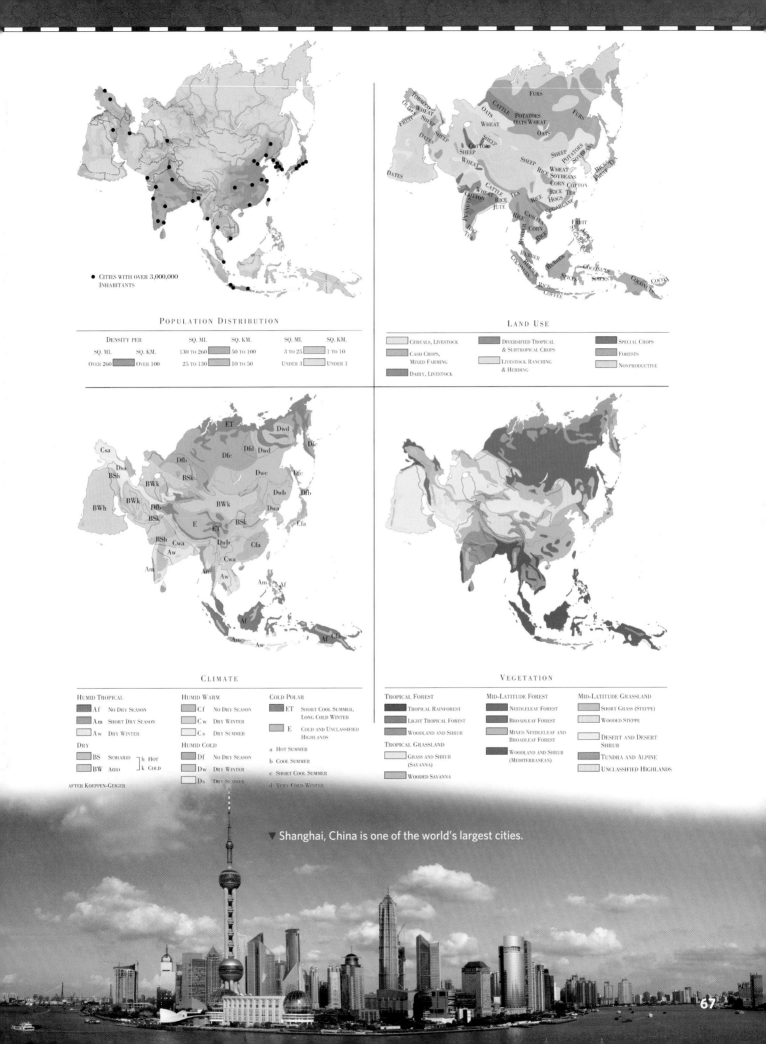

POPULATION DISTRIBUTION

● CITIES WITH OVER 3,000,000 INHABITANTS

DENSITY PER							
SQ. MI.	SQ. KM.	SQ. MI.	SQ. KM.	SQ. MI.	SQ. KM.	SQ. MI.	SQ. KM.
OVER 260	OVER 100	130 TO 260	50 TO 100			3 TO 25	1 TO 10
		25 TO 130	10 TO 50			UNDER 3	UNDER 1

LAND USE

CEREALS, LIVESTOCK	DIVERSIFIED TROPICAL & SUBTROPICAL CROPS
CASH CROPS, MIXED FARMING	LIVESTOCK RANCHING & HERDING
DAIRY, LIVESTOCK	

SPECIAL CROPS
FORESTS
NONPRODUCTIVE

CLIMATE

HUMID TROPICAL
Af NO DRY SEASON
Am SHORT DRY SEASON
Aw DRY WINTER

DRY
BS SEMIARID ⎫ h HOT
BW ARID   ⎭ k COLD

AFTER KOEPPEN-GEIGER

HUMID WARM
Cf NO DRY SEASON
Cw DRY WINTER
Cs DRY SUMMER

HUMID COLD
Df NO DRY SEASON
Dw DRY WINTER
Ds DRY SUMMER

COLD POLAR
ET SHORT COOL SUMMER, LONG COLD WINTER
E COLD AND UNCLASSIFIED HIGHLANDS

a HOT SUMMER
b COOL SUMMER
c SHORT COOL SUMMER
d VERY COLD WINTER

VEGETATION

TROPICAL FOREST
TROPICAL RAINFOREST
LIGHT TROPICAL FOREST
WOODLAND AND SHRUB

TROPICAL GRASSLAND
GRASS AND SHRUB (SAVANNA)
WOODED SAVANNA

MID-LATITUDE FOREST
NEEDLELEAF FOREST
BROADLEAF FOREST
MIXED NEEDLELEAF AND BROADLEAF FOREST
WOODLAND AND SHRUB (MEDITERRANEAN)

MID-LATITUDE GRASSLAND
SHORT GRASS (STEPPE)
WOODED STEPPE
DESERT AND DESERT SHRUB
TUNDRA AND ALPINE
UNCLASSIFIED HIGHLANDS

▼ Shanghai, China is one of the world's largest cities.

ASIA
POLITICAL MAP

Scale of Miles
0 200 400 600 800 1000

Scale of Kilometers
0 300 600 900 1200 1500

NORTH AMERICA

ARCTIC OCEAN

180°
160°
140°
120°
100°
80°
60°
40°
20°
0°

A B C D E F G H J

EUROPE

PACIFIC OCEAN

Bering Sea

Kolyma R.

Kamchatka Pen.

Lena R.

Siberia

Angara R.

Yenisey R.

Ob' River

Ural Mountains

Zhayyq R.

Tobol R.

Irtysh R.

Ob' R.

Aldan R.

Amur R.

L. Baykal

SEA OF OKHOTSK

Sakhalin

Kuril Is.

Hokkaidō

Arctic Circle

Black Sea

CAUCASUS

Mt. Ararat 5,165 m

Zagros Mountains

Tigris R.

Euphrates R.

Caspian Sea

Aral Sea

Syrdariya R.

Amu Darya R.

Lake Balkhash

Altai Mtns.

Gobi Desert

Tarin R.

Kunlun Mountains

Huang (Yellow) R.

Chang R. (Yangtze)

SEA OF JAPAN

Honshū

EAST CHINA SEA

Red Sea

Arabian Peninsula

Persian Gulf

Gulf of Oman

Indus R.

Himalaya

Mt. Everest 8,848 m

Ganges R.

Xi R.

Taiwan

North Tropic Line (Tropic of Cancer)

Gulf of Aden

ARABIAN SEA

Godāvari R.

WESTERN GHATS

BAY OF BENGAL

Andaman Sea

Ayeyarwady R.

Salween R.

Mekong R.

Indochinese Peninsula

SOUTH CHINA SEA

Luzon

PHILIPPINE ISLANDS

AFRICA

Ceylon (Sri Lanka)

Maldive Islands

Malay Peninsula

Borneo

Celebes

0° Equator

INDIAN OCEAN

Equator

Seychelles

Sumatra

Java

Timor

SUNDA ISLANDS

Madagascar

South Tropic Line (Tropic of Capricorn)

AUSTRALIA

68

B 60° C 80° Longitude East of Greenwich 100° E

© HAMMOND WORLD ATLAS CORPORATION

AUSTRALIA THE SMALLEST CONTINENT

Koala

Australia is Earth's smallest continent. It lies southeast of Asia, between the Indian and Pacific Oceans. Australia, like an island, is completely surrounded by water. But Australia is over three times larger than the world's largest island, Greenland.

All of Australia is south of the equator. In fact, the name comes from the Latin word for "south". Many people refer to Australia as "the land down under", because it is at the "bottom" of the earth. Seasons are the opposite of those in the Northern Hemisphere. Winter begins in June and summer starts in December.

Australia's climate is warm and dry. Mild winters bring snow only to the highest mountains. These are found in the east. The Great Dividing Range runs the length of the continent. West of this range are the Central Lowlands. Little rain falls here and lakes often dry up completely. The Western Plateau extends to the Indian Ocean. It is flat and dry, either desert or arid grassland. Few people live west of the Great Dividing Range, except for some farmlands along the coasts.

Most Australians live in the cities along the southeast coast. This is one of the areas with good farmland. City people call the huge, dry interior of Australia "the outback". The dry grasslands are used for raising sheep and cattle. Wool is a major export. Wheat is Australia's major crop.

Many unique animals, such as the kangaroo, koala and platypus, are found only here. These are **marsupials**, mammals that have a pouch to carry their young. Off the east coast lies the Great Barrier Reef. It's the largest coral reef in the world and is home to thousands of kinds of fish.

The original natives of Australia are known as the Aborigines. People from Great Britain began arriving more than 200 years ago. Today, English is spoken and most people have a European heritage. Australia is the Earth's only continent to have just one nation.

Many maps show New Zealand with Australia. This island nation lies southeast of Australia. Both North and South Islands, the two largest, have rugged mountains and a cool climate. The British also settled in New Zealand, and English is spoken here too. Sheep are raised and wool is the major export.

Look at the map on page 73. When British settlers arrived in New Zealand, they found Maoris, a Polynesian people, already living there. These people came from Polynesia many years ago. Along with Melanesia and Micronesia, Polynesia is part of the Pacific Ocean called **Oceania**. This is a vast area of small islands, many far from the next. It even includes the Hawaiian Islands, the fiftieth state of the United States.

CONTINENT CLOSEUP

- Nine of every ten Australians live in cities or towns.

- Koalas are not bears. They are marsupials that feed on eucalyptus trees and shoots, and drink no water.

- Edward Eyre was the first person to cross the continent in 1841.

- Most of the Great Barrier Reef is a National Park. Taking coral from the reef is strictly forbidden.

▼ Wheat is Australia's main agricultural product. It is grown on about half of Australia's farmland. Sheep-raising is another important occupation.

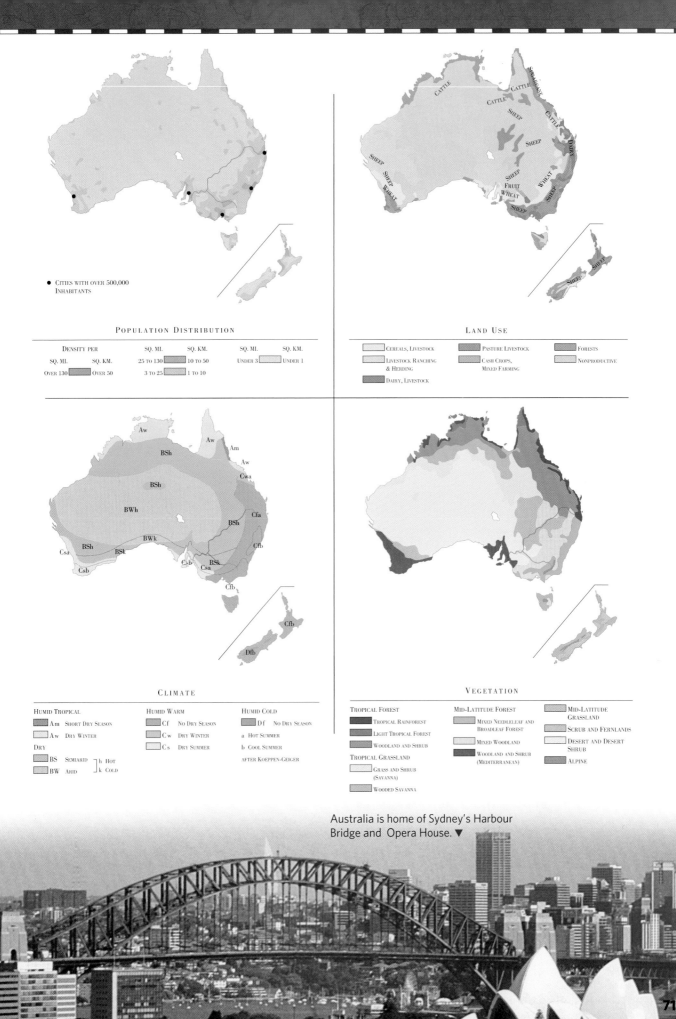

● CITIES WITH OVER 500,000 INHABITANTS

POPULATION DISTRIBUTION

DENSITY PER						
SQ. MI.	SQ. KM.	SQ. MI. 25 TO 130	SQ. KM. 10 TO 50	SQ. MI. UNDER 3	SQ. KM. UNDER 1	
OVER 130	OVER 50	3 TO 25	1 TO 10			

LAND USE

- CEREALS, LIVESTOCK
- LIVESTOCK RANCHING & HERDING
- DAIRY, LIVESTOCK
- PASTURE LIVESTOCK
- CASH CROPS, MIXED FARMING
- FORESTS
- NONPRODUCTIVE

CLIMATE

HUMID TROPICAL
- Am SHORT DRY SEASON
- Aw DRY WINTER

DRY
- BS SEMIARID
- BW ARID
  - h HOT
  - k COLD

HUMID WARM
- Cf NO DRY SEASON
- Cw DRY WINTER
- Cs DRY SUMMER

HUMID COLD
- Df NO DRY SEASON
- a HOT SUMMER
- b COOL SUMMER

AFTER KOEPPEN-GEIGER

VEGETATION

TROPICAL FOREST
- TROPICAL RAINFOREST
- LIGHT TROPICAL FOREST
- WOODLAND AND SHRUB

TROPICAL GRASSLAND
- GRASS AND SHRUB (SAVANNA)
- WOODED SAVANNA

MID-LATITUDE FOREST
- MIXED NEEDLELEAF AND BROADLEAF FOREST
- MIXED WOODLAND
- WOODLAND AND SHRUB (MEDITERRANEAN)

MID-LATITUDE GRASSLAND
- SCRUB AND FERNLANDS
- DESERT AND DESERT SHRUB
- ALPINE

Australia is home of Sydney's Harbour Bridge and Opera House. ▼

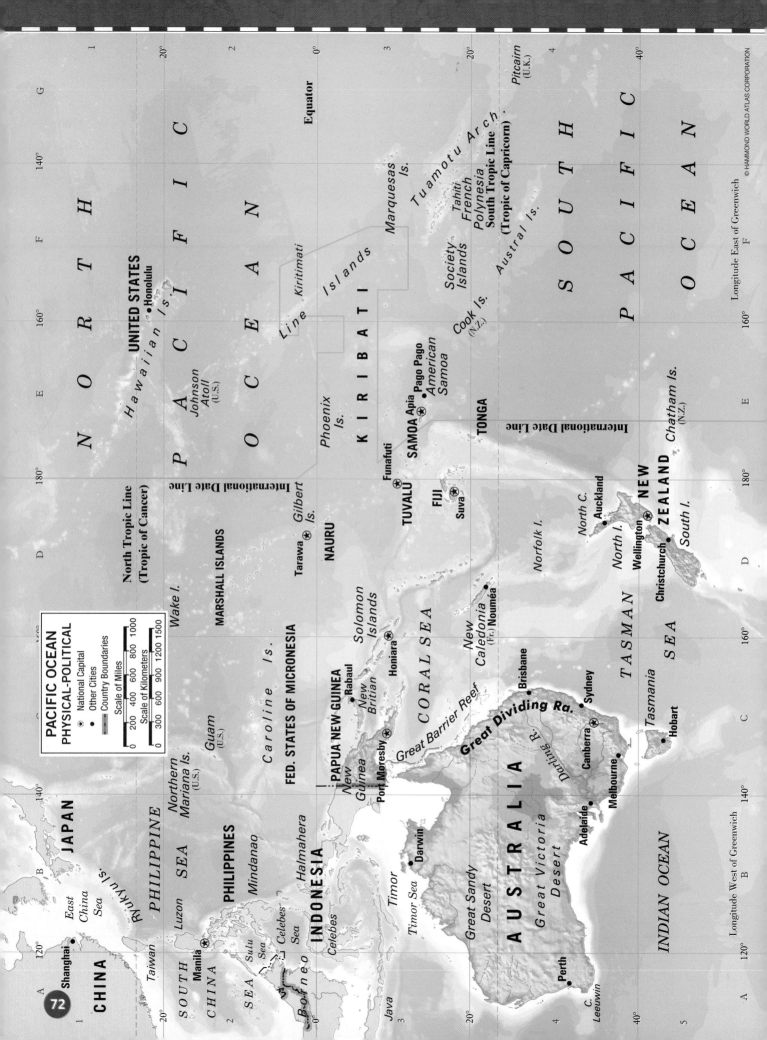

PACIFIC OCEAN
PHYSICAL-POLITICAL

⊛ National Capital
• Other Cities
━━━ Country Boundaries

Scale of Miles
0 200 400 600 800 1000

Scale of Kilometers
0 300 600 900 1200 1500

© HAMMOND WORLD ATLAS CORPORATION

JAPAN

East China Sea

Ryukyu Is.

Taiwan

CHINA
• Shanghai

PHILIPPINE SEA

Luzon

Northern Mariana Is. (U.S.)

PHILIPPINES
⊛ Manila

Mindanao

Guam (U.S.)

Sulu Sea

Celebes Sea

Celebes

B o r n e o

INDONESIA

Halmahera

Java

Timor

Timor Sea

• Darwin

Great Sandy Desert

Great Victoria Desert

A U S T R A L I A

C. Leeuwin

• Perth

Adelaide •

Darling R.

Great Dividing Ra.

Canberra ⊛

Melbourne •

Sydney •

• Brisbane

CORAL SEA

Great Barrier Reef

Tasmania

• Hobart

TASMAN SEA

New Caledonia (Fr.)
• Nouméa

Norfolk I.

NEW ZEALAND

North I.

North C.

• Auckland

Wellington ⊛

Christchurch •

South I.

Chatham Is. (N.Z.)

INDIAN OCEAN

Longitude West of Greenwich

Longitude East of Greenwich

FED. STATES OF MICRONESIA

Caroline Is.

PAPUA NEW GUINEA

New Guinea

Port Moresby ⊛

Rabaul •

New Britian

Solomon Islands

Honiara ⊛

MARSHALL ISLANDS

Wake I.

North Tropic Line
(Tropic of Cancer)

International Date Line

Tarawa ⊛

Gilbert Is.

NAURU

K I R I B A T I

Phoenix Is.

Line Islands

Kiritimati

Funafuti •

TUVALU

Suva •

FIJI

TONGA

Apia
SAMOA ⊛

Pago Pago •
American Samoa

International Date Line

Equator

Marquesas Is.

Tuamotu Arch.

Tahiti
French Polynesia

South Tropic Line
(Tropic of Capricorn)

Society Islands

Austral Is.

Cook Is. (N.Z.)

Pitcairn (U.K.)

S O U T H

P A C I F I C

O C E A N

UNITED STATES

Hawaiian Is.

• Honolulu

Johnson Atoll (U.S.)

N O R T H

P A C I F I C

O C E A N

S O U T H   C H I N A   S E A

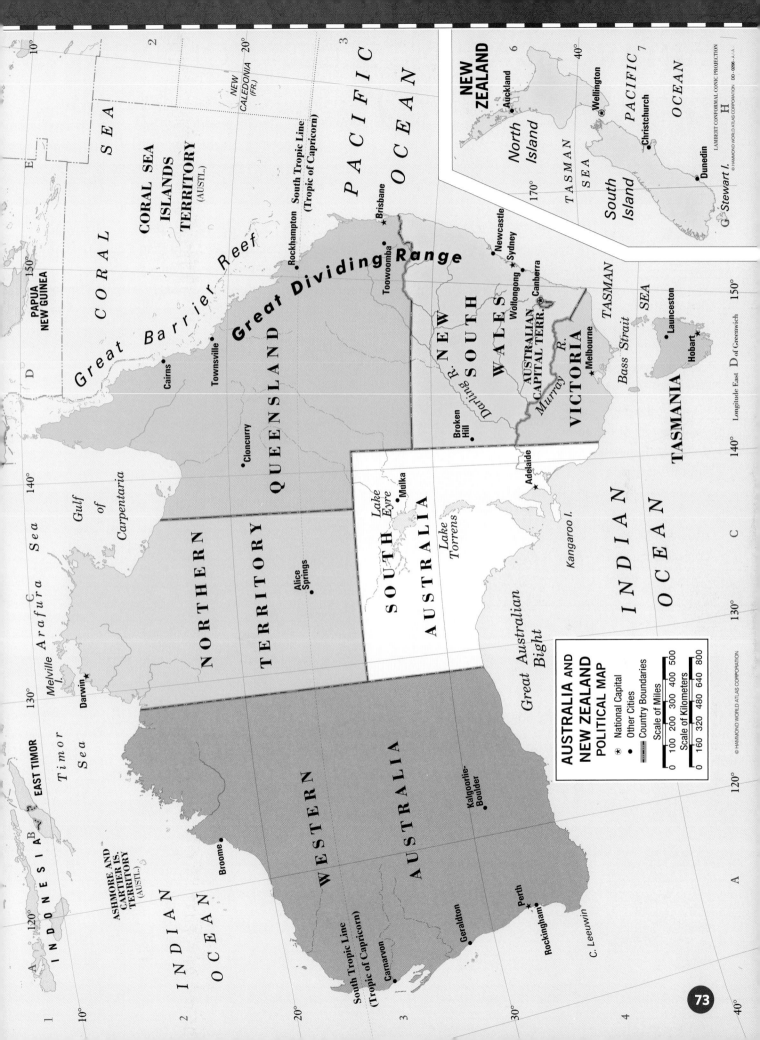

NEW ZEALAND

Auckland

North Island

TASMAN

SEA

170°

40°

Wellington

PACIFIC

Christchurch

Dunedin

South Island

OCEAN

G Stewart I.

LAMBERT CONFORMAL CONIC PROJECTION

DD-0206-A-I-A

© HAMMOND WORLD ATLAS CORPORATION

PAPUA
NEW GUINEA

150°

NEW
CALEDONIA
(FR.)

2

20°

CORAL SEA
ISLANDS
TERRITORY
(AUSTL.)

South Tropic Line
(Tropic of Capricorn)

PACIFIC

3

CORAL SEA

Great Barrier Reef

Rockhampton

Brisbane

OCEAN

Great Dividing Range

Toowoomba

Newcastle

Sydney

INDONESIA

EAST TIMOR

120°

10°

Timor
Sea

130°

Melville
I.

Arafura
Sea

Darwin

Gulf
of
Carpentaria

140°

Cairns

Townsville

QUEENSLAND

Cloncurry

Wollongong

Canberra

NEW

SOUTH

WALES

AUSTRALIAN
CAPITAL TERR.

Darling R.

Murray R.

Broken
Hill

VICTORIA

Melbourne

TASMAN

SEA

Bass Strait

Launceston

Hobart

TASMANIA

150°

Longitude East D of Greenwich

C

140°

NORTHERN

TERRITORY

Alice
Springs

Adelaide

SOUTH

AUSTRALIA

Lake
Eyre

Mulka

Lake
Torrens

Kangaroo I.

INDIAN

OCEAN

130°

ASHMORE AND
CARTIER IS.
TERRITORY
(AUSTL.)

INDIAN

OCEAN

Broome

WESTERN

AUSTRALIA

Kalgoorlie-
Boulder

Great Australian
Bight

120°

40°

Geraldton

Carnarvon

South Tropic Line
(Tropic of Capricorn)

Perth

Rockingham

C. Leeuwin

30°

AUSTRALIA AND
NEW ZEALAND
POLITICAL MAP

⊛ National Capital
• Other Cities
▬▬▬ Country Boundaries

Scale of Miles

0 100 200 300 400 500

Scale of Kilometers

0 160 320 480 640 800

© HAMMOND WORLD ATLAS CORPORATION

ANTARCTICA THE COLDEST CONTINENT

Penguins

Antarctica is the southernmost continent on Earth. In size, Antarctica is smaller than South America, but larger than Europe. The southern edges of the Pacific, Atlantic and Indian Oceans surround Antarctica.

Many maps make Antarctica appear huge. Look at the world map on pages 38-39. To show the round world on a flat map, some areas are distorted from their real shapes. Compare Antarctica on the map below. This map is a type of polar projection. It is centered on the South Pole, instead of the equator. On this map, the size and shape of Antarctica is truer to the way it actually is.

East Antarctica is a high plateau. Most of the western half of the continent is below sea level. The Antarctic Peninsula extends like a finger toward South America. Experts think the mountains here are an extension of the Andes range.

Very little of Antarctica's land can be seen. Ice and snow a mile thick covers the land. It is the coldest continent on Earth. There is more fresh water in this ice cap than on all six other continents combined. Antarctica's climate is very dry. Cold, bitter winds whip across the continent. In spring, icebergs break off from the edges of the icecap. Animals, such as seals and penguins, live at the coasts, feeding on fish. The climate is too cold for any food crops.

Antarctica has no permanent settlers. It is the last continent to be explored. More than a dozen nations have scientific stations here. Many nations are interested in the natural resources that may lie under Antarctica's frozen surface.

CONTINENT CLOSEUP

- In Wilkes Land, the ice cap is more than three miles thick.

- A Norwegian group, led by Roald Amundsen, was the first group to reach the South Pole in 1911.

- Whales migrate here in summer to feed on krill in the offshore waters.

- Much of west Antarctica is below sea level. If the ice cap melted, this area would be a chain of islands in a vast sea.

© HAMMOND WORLD ATLAS CORPORATION

CONTINENT COMPARISONS

ASIA

AREA 17,128,500 sq. mi.
44,362,815 sq. km.
POPULATION 4,004,788,000

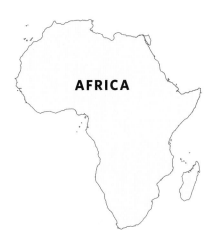

AFRICA

AREA 11,707,000 sq. mi.
30,321,130 sq. km.
POPULATION 935,813,000

NORTH AMERICA

AREA 9,363,000 sq. mi.
24,250,170 sq. km.
POPULATION 523,686,000

SOUTH AMERICA

AREA 6,879,725 sq. mi.
17,818,505 sq. km.
POPULATION 380,017,000

ANTARCTICA

AREA 5,405,000 sq. mi.
14,000,000 sq. km.
POPULATION No permanent
population

EUROPE

AREA 4,057,000 sq. mi.
10,507,630 sq. km.
POPULATION 727,228,000

AUSTRALIA

AREA
2,967,893 sq. mi.
7,686,850 sq. km.
POPULATION 20,434,000

GEOGRAPHIC COMPARISONS

Ellesmere ⑩

Victoria ⑨

Greenland ①

ASIA

Arctic Circle

Mt. McKinley
20,320 ⑨

GREAT BEAR
LAKE

Baffin ⑤

Great Britain ⑧

NORTH

② LAKE SUPERIOR

④ LAKE HURON

Death Valley
-282

Mississippi-
Missouri 3

⑤ LAKE MICHIGAN

AMERICA

Tropic of Cancer

Equator

Amazon 2

SOUTH

AMERICA

Tropic of Capricorn

Cerro Aconcagua
22,831

Salina Grande (Pen. Valés)
-131

Antarctic Circle

Vinson Massif
16,864

■ Sea Level

A N T A R

KEY TO SYMBOLS ON MAP

▲ Highest Point of Continent (in feet)

■ Lowest Point of Continent (in feet)

① Ten Largest Islands of the World

① Ten Largest Lakes of the World

1 Ten Longest Rivers of the World

EUROPE

Yenisey-Angara 6

Lena 9

Ob'-Irtysh 5

LAKE BAYKAL
8

Caspian Sea
-92 6

ARAL SEA

A

Amur-
Shilka-
Onon 8

El'brus
18,510

1

CASPIAN SEA

S

I

Honshu
7

Dead Sea
-1,329

Mt. Everest
29,028

Huang 7

A

Chang 4

1
Nile

R I C A

Lake Assal
-512

LAKE VICTORIA
3

Kilimanjaro 19,340

Congo
10

7 LAKE TANGANYIKA

Borneo
3

New Guinea
2

10 LAKE NYASA

Sumatra
6

Madagascar
4

AUSTRALIA

Lake Eyre
-52

Mt. Kosciusko
7,310

C T I C A

Scale of Miles
0 300 600 900 1200 1500
Scale of Kilometers
0 500 1000 1500 2000 2500

© HAMMOND WORLD ATLAS CORPORATION

WHERE IN **THE WORLD**

	Highest Places	Lowest Places	Driest Places
North America	Mount McKinley, Alaska 20,320 feet	Death Valley, California* 282 feet below sea level	Batagues, Mexico one inch of rain a year
South America	Aconcagua, Argentina* 22,831 feet	Valdés Peninsula, Argentina 131 feet below sea level	Atacama Desert, Chile rain only two to four times a century
Africa	Kilimanjaro, Tanzania* 19,340 feet	Lake Assal, Djibouti 512 feet below sea level	Wadi Halfa, Sudan less than one-tenth of an inch of rain a year
Europe	Mount Elbrus, Russia* 18,510 feet	Caspian Sea, Russia 92 feet below sea level	Astrakhan, Russia six inches of rain a year
Asia	Mount Everest, Nepal/China 29,028 feet	Dead Sea, Israel/Jordan* 1,338 feet below sea level	Aden, Yemen two inches of rain a year
Australia and the Pacific	Mauna Kea, Hawaii 13,796 feet Mt. Kosciusko, Australia 7,310 feet	Lake Eyre, Australia* 52 feet below sea level	Mulka, Australia four inches of rain a year
Antarctica	Vinson Massif 16,864 feet	Unknown	South Pole Station* less than one inch of snow a year

See photo at the beginning of the column.

Wettest Places	Warmest Places	Coldest Places
Henderson Lake, Canada 256 inches of rain a year	**Death Valley, California** 134 degrees F., July 10, 1913 **Yuma, Arizona** 107 degrees F., average daily high in July	**Northice, Greenland** -87 degrees F., Jan. 9, 1954 **Eismitte, Greenland** -41 degrees F., average daily low in January
Quibdo, Colombia 354 inches of rain a year	**Rivadavia, Argentina** 120 degrees F., average daily high in July **Santiago del Estero, Argentina** 97 degrees F., average daily high in January	**Sarmiento, Argentina** -27 degrees F., June 1, 1907 **La Quiaca, Argentina** 16 degrees F., average daily low in July
Debundscha, Cameroon 405 inches of rain a year	**Al'Aziziyah, Libya** 136 degrees F., Sept. 13, 1922 **Adrar, Algeria** 115 degrees F., average daily high in July	**Ifrane, Morocco** -11 degrees F., Feb. 11, 1935 **Tshabong, Botswana** 37 degrees F., average daily low in July
Crkvica, Bosnia and Herzegovina 183 inches of rain a year	**Seville, Spain** 122 degrees F., August 4, 1881 **Seville, Spain** 97 degrees F., average daily high in August	**Ust'Shchugor, Russia** -67 degrees F., date unknown **Ust'Shchugor, Russia** -14 degrees F., average daily low in January
Cherrapunji, India 450 inches of rain a year	**Tirat Zevi, Israel** 129 degrees F., June 21, 1942 **Abadan, Iran** 112 degrees F., average daily high in July	**Verkhoyansk, Russia** -90 degrees F., Feb. 7, 1892 **Verkhoyansk, Russia** -58 degrees F., average daily low in January
Mount Waialeale, Hawaii 460 inches of rain a year **Tully, Australia** 160 inches of rain a year	**Cloncurry, Australia** 128 degrees F., January 16, 1889 **Mundiwindi, Australia** 101 degrees F., average daily high in January	**Charlotte Pass, Australia** -9 degrees F., June 29, 1994 **Canberra, Australia** 32 degrees F., average daily low in July
Unknown	**Vanda, Scott Coast** 59 degrees F., January 5, 1974	**Vostok Station** -128 degrees F., July 21, 1983

Temperatures shown in degrees Fahrenheit.

WHERE IN **THE WORLD**

	Longest Rivers	Major Lakes	Waterfalls
North America	Mississippi-Missouri, United States 3,710 miles	Superior, USA/Canada 31,700 square miles Huron, USA/Canada 23,000 square miles Michigan, USA 22,300 square miles	Yosemite, California* 2,425-foot drop (3 steps) Ribbon, California 1,612-foot drop Niagara, USA/Canada 173-foot drop
South America	Amazon, Brazil/Peru 4,000 miles	Titicaca, Peru/Bolivia* 3,200 square miles	Angel, Venezuela 3,212-foot drop (2 steps) Cequenan, Venezuela 2,000-foot drop Iguaçu, Argentina/Brazil 237-foot drop
Africa	Nile, Egypt/Sudan/ Uganda/Burundi 4,160 miles	Victoria, Kenya/ Uganda/Tanzania 26,830 square miles Tanganyika, Burundi/Dem. Rep. of the Congo/ Tanzania/Zambia 12,700 square miles	Tugela, South Africa 3,110-foot drop (5 steps) Victoria, Zimbabwe/Zambia* 343-foot drop
Europe	Volga, Russia* 2,290 miles	Caspian Sea 143,240 square miles Ladoga, Russia 6,900 square miles	Balåifossen, Norway 2,788-foot drop Ramnefjellsfossen, Norway 2,685-foot drop
Asia	Chang Jiang (Yangtze), China 3,960 miles	Caspian Sea 143,240 square miles Aral Sea, Kazakhstan/ Uzbekistan 15,830 square miles Baykal, Russia 12,160 square miles	Barehipani, India 1,309-foot drop Nam Tok Karom, Thailand: 1,300-foot drop
Australia and the Pacific	Murray-Darling, Australia 2,310 miles	Eyre, Australia 3,000 square miles	Sutherland, N. Z. 1,904-foot drop (3 steps)
Antarctica	None	None	None

See photo at the beginning of the column.

Major Islands	Active Volcanoes
Greenland: 840,000 square miles **Baffin:** 195,928 square miles **Victoria:** 83,897 square miles **Ellesmere:** 75,767 square miles **Newfoundland:** 42,031 square miles **Cuba:** 42,804 square miles	**Mt. St. Helens, Washington:** erupted in 1980 **Mount Irazu, Costa Rica:** erupted in 1965 **Soufriere Hills, Montserrat:** erupted in 1995 **Popocateptl, Mexico:** erupted in 1996 **Mount Redoubt, Alaska:** erupted in 1990 **Colima, Mexico:** erupted in 2005
Tierra del Fuego: 18,301 square miles **Marajó:** 17,991 square miles	**Nevado del Ruiz, Colombia:** erupted in 1985 **Galeras Volcano, Colombia:** erupted in 2008 **Guagua Pichincha, Ecuador:** erupted in 1998 **Llaima, Chile:** erupted in 2004 **Cotopaxi, Ecuador:** erupted in 1940 **Fernandina, Galapagos Is.:** erupted in 1995
Madagascar: 226,657 square miles	**Cameroon Mountain, Cameroon:** erupted in 1999 **Ol Doinyo Lengai, Tanzania:** erupted in 2006 **Nyiragongo, Dem. Rep. of the Congo:** erupted in 2002 **Nyamuragira, Dem. Rep. of the Congo:** erupted in 2004
Great Britain: 84,400 square miles **Iceland:** 39,768 square miles **Ireland:** 27,136 square miles	**Mount Etna, Italy:** erupted in 2007 **Stromboli, Italy:** erupted in 2007 **Mount Vesuvius, Italy:** erupted in 1944 **Surtsey, Iceland:** erupted in 1967 **Loki, Iceland:** erupted in 1910
New Guinea: 305,000 square miles **Borneo:** 286,000 square miles **Sumatra:** 164,000 square miles **Honshu:** 88,000 square miles **Java:** 48,842 square miles **Luzon:** 40,420 square miles	**Klyuchevskaya Sopka, Russia:** erupted in 2007 **Mount Kerinci, Indonesia:** erupted in 2004 **Mount Pinatubo, Philippines:** erupted in 1993 **On-Take, Japan:** erupted in 1980 **Unzen Volcano, Japan:** erupted in 1991 **Mount Merapi, Indonesia:*** erupted in 2006
New Guinea: 305,000 square miles **South Island, N. Z.:** 58,393 square miles **North Island, N. Z.:** 44,187 square miles **Tasmania:** 26,410 square miles **New Britain:** 14,100 square miles	**Manam, Papua New Guinea:** erupted in 2004 **McDonald Island, Australia:** erupted in 2001 **Mount Ulawun, New Britain:** erupted in 2005 **Kilauea, Hawaii:** erupted in 1990 **Mauna Loa, Hawaii:** erupted in 1984 **Ruapehu, New Zealand:*** erupted in 2007
Alexander: 16,700 square miles	**Big Ben, Heard Island:** erupted in 2001 **Mount Erebus, Ross Island:*** erupted in 2005

WHERE IN THE WORLD

	Reptiles & Amphibians		Birds	
North America	Rattlesnakes Corn Snake Copperhead Water Moccasin Coral Snake King Snake	Bullfrog Box Turtle Horned Lizard Alligator Gila Monster Skink	Turkey Mourning Dove Canada Goose Robin Roadrunner Burrowing Owl	Prairie Chicken Cardinal* Wood Duck Loon Snowy Egret Bald Eagle
South America	Boa Constrictor Anaconda Bushmaster Fer-de-lance	Horned Frog Galapagos Tortoise Spectacled Caiman Iguana Surinam Toad	Rhea Keel-billed Toucan Cock-of-the-Rock Hummingbird Tinamou Macaw	Potoo Flamingo Scarlet Ibis Andean Condor Hoatzin
Africa	Black Mamba Rock Python Ringhals (Spitting Cobra) African Egg Eater Gaboon Viper Boomslang	Crocodile Nile Monitor Chameleon Clawed Frog Plated Lizard Goliath Frog	Ostrich Secretary Bird Lanner Falcon Vulture Emerald Cuckoo Shoebill	Flamingo Touraco Helmet Bird Weaverbird Oxpecker
Europe	Cross Adder Grass Snake Asp	Green Tree Frog Pond Turtle Alpine Newt Fire Salamander European Toad Greek Tortoise	Skylark White Stork* House Sparrow Nightingale Brambling Wall Creeper	Imperial Eagle Grey Wagtail Blackcap Ring Ouzel Raven Jay
Asia	King Cobra Tree Snake Russell's Viper Reticulated Python Banded Krait	Komodo Dragon Salt-water Crocodile Gavial Mandarin Newt Hardun Flying Dragon	Mandarin Duck Golden Pheasant Peacock Fruit Dove Brahminy Kite Tailorbird	Rhinoceros Hornbill Himalayan Monal Red Jungle Fowl Magpie Sarus Crane
Australia and the Pacific	Tiger Snake Taipan Australian Brown Snake Death Adder Sea Snakes	Moloch Lizard Frilled Lizard Gecko Bearded Dragon Skink White's Frog	Cockatoo Emu Kookaburra Black Swan Lyrebird	Budgerigar Regent Bowerbird Grey Butcherbird Blue Wren
Antarctica	Sea Snakes		Emperor Penguin Storm Petrel*	Albatross Skua

* See photo at the beginning of the column.

Mammals			Trees		Gems
Canadian Otter	Jack Rabbit	Chipmunk	Douglas Fir	Sequoia	Turquoise
Grizzly Bear	Raccoon	Bison	White Pine	Maple	Aquamarine
White-tailed Deer	Porcupine	Beaver	Magnolia	Hemlock	Jade
Bighorn Sheep	Caribou	Puma	Sweet Gum	Hickory	Tourmaline
Grey Squirrel	Coyote	Muskrat	Redwood		Agate
Striped Skunk					Peridot
Brazilian Tapir	Guinea Pig	Jaguar	Jacaranda	Balsa	Diamond
Giant Armadillo	Vampire Bat	Ocelot	Mahogany	Cashew	Amethyst
Giant Anteater	Marmoset	Opossum	Brazil Nut	Southern Beech	Tourmaline
Two-toed Sloth	Capuchin	Llama	Logwood		Aquamarine
Chinchilla	Alpaca★				Emerald
					Topaz
					Onyx
Hippopotamus	Lion	Baboon	Yellow-wood	Rosewood	Diamond
Rhinoceros	Honey Badger	Impala	Date Palm	Baobab	Emerald
Chimpanzee	Wart Hog	Lemur	African Tulip	Cedar	Tourmaline
Giraffe	Cheetah	Zebra	Cork Oak	Ebony	Garnet
Dromedary	African Elephant★	Hyena	Mangrove	Oil Palm	
(Camel)	Gorilla				
Red Deer	Mouflon		Chestnut	Pine	Topaz
House Mouse	Weasel		Juniper	Beech	Garnet
Wild Boar	Moose		Walnut	Yew	
Red Fox	Chamois		Cork Oak	Plain	
Reindeer			Spruce	Oak	
Indian Elephant	Mongoose	Leopard	Eastern Spruce	Sandalwood	Diamond
Bactrian Camel	Gibbon	Wolf	Rhododendron	Banyan	Ruby
Orangutan	Yak	Tiger★	Cherry	Larch	Emerald
Rhesus Monkey	Blackbuck	Sable	Mango	Teak	Jade
Water Buffalo	Giant Panda	Lemming	Mulberry	Rubber	Zircon
					Sapphire
					Moonstone
Tasmanian	Wombat		Eucalyptus	Snow Gum	Sapphire
Devil	Koala		White Mallee	Silk Oak	Opal
Duck-billed	Dingo		Wattle	Desert	Pearl
Platypus			Blue Gum	Kurrajong	
Kangaroo★					
Sea Lion			None		None
Whales					

83

WHERE IN THE WORLD

	Principal Cities		Landmarks From the Past
North America 	New York, New York Mexico, Mexico Los Angeles, California Chicago, Illinois Philadelphia, Pennsylvania Toronto, Canada★		**Pyramid of the Moon, Teotihuacán, Mexico** built in 900–1100 **Anasazi Pueblo Bonito, New Mexico** built about 1050 **Chichén Itzá, Mexico** abandoned in 1400s
South America 	São Paulo, Brazil Buenos Aires, Argentina Rio de Janiero, Brazil Caracas, Venezuela Bogotá, Colombia Lima, Peru		**Royal Road of the Incas, Andes Mountains** built in 1200–1500 **Machu Picchu, Peru**★ built in 1200-1500 **Chan Chan, Peru** built in 1000-1400
Africa 	Cairo, Egypt Lagos, Nigeria Johannesburg, South Africa		**The Sphinx and Giza Pyramids, Egypt**★ begun about 2500 B.C. **Temple of Ramses II, Egypt** built about 1250 B.C. **Great Zimbabwe ruins, Zimbabwe** built in 1000-1400
Europe 	London, England Paris, France Moscow, Russia Berlin, Germany St. Petersburg, Russia	Madrid, Spain Milan, Italy Rome, Italy Athens, Greece Istanbul, Turkey	**Acropolis of Athens, Greece**★ begun in 400s B.C. **Colosseum of Rome, Italy** begun about 70 B.C. **Stonehenge ruins, England** built 1800-1400 B.C.
Asia 	Tokyo, Japan Shanghai, China Beijing, China Calcutta, India Seoul, Korea Taipei, Taiwan	Jakarta, Indonesia Mumbai, India Manila, Philippines Karachi, Pakistan Bangkok, Thailand Tehran, Iran	**Dome of the Rock, Jerusalem** begun in 691 **Great Wall of China**★ begun about 200 B.C. **Taj Mahal, India** built in 1600s
Australia and the Pacific 	Sydney, Australia Melbourne, Australia Honolulu, Hawaii		**Caves of Uluru, or Ayers Rock, Australia**★ dates unknown **Giant Statues, Easter Island, Chile** origin unknown
Antarctica	None		Unknown

★ See photo at the beginning of the column.

Modern Engineering Marvels		Tallest Buildings
Delaware Tunnel, NY State, USA: 85-mile water tunnel, world's longest **CN Tower, Toronto, Canada** 1,815-foot tower **KVLY-TV Tower, Blanchard, ND, USA** 2,063 feet tall, world's tallest structure	**Panama Canal, Panama** 51-mile waterway, opened 1914, connects Atlantic and Pacific **Lake Pontchartrain Causeway, Louisiana, USA:** 24 miles long, world's longest bridge	**Sears Tower, Chicago, Illinois** 1,454 feet **Empire State Building, New York, N.Y.** 1,250 feet
Itaipu Hydroelectric Dam, Paraná River, Brazil/Paraguay the continent's largest waterpower project		**Parque Central Torre Officinas, Caracas, Venezuela** 725 feet
Lake Volta, Ghana 3,275 square miles, world's largest artificial lake **Kimberley Mine, South Africa** over 3000-foot deep, 1500-foot wide pit, world's largest excavation	**Aswan High Dam, Nile River, Egypt** over two-and-a-half miles long, 364 feet high **Suez Canal, Egypt:** opened 1869 100 miles long, connects Red and Mediterranean Seas	**Carlton Centre, Johannesburg, South Africa** 730 feet
Humber Bridge, England 4,626 foot suspension span **Eiffel Tower, Paris, France** 1,063 feet tall, opened 1889 **Channel Tunnel, England/France** world's longest undersea tunnel		**Commerzbank, Frankfurt, Germany:** 985 feet **Messeturm Building, Frankfurt, Germany:** 843 feet **Moscow State University, Moscow, Russia:** 787 feet
Akashi-Kaikyo Bridge, Japan 6,532-foot suspension span, world's longest single span **Seikan Rail Tunnel, Japan** over 33 miles, world's longest rail tunnel	**Rogun Dam, Vakhsh River, Tajikistan** 1,066 feet tall, world's highest dam **Grand Canal, China** 1,100 miles long, world's longest canal system **Three Gorges Dam, China** world's largest hydroelectric dam	**Taiwan 101 Tower, T'aipei, Taiwan:** 1,670 feet **Petronas Towers, Kuala Lumpur, Malaysia:** 1,483 feet **Jin Mao Building, Shanghai, China:** 1,381 feet
Trans-Australian Railroad, Australia 298 miles of straight track in one stretch		**Eureka Tower, Melbourne, Australia** 975 feet **Rialto Tower, Melbourne, Australia** 886 feet **MLC Centre, Sydney, Australia** 800 feet
Not applicable		Not applicable

WHERE IN **THE WORLD**

Food Specialties

North America

Barbados: Cou-cou (cornmeal and okra)
Jamaica: Jerk Pork (cured pork strips)
Mexico: Tortillas (corn pancakes) and Tamales (cornmeal and meat)

Panama: Guacho (rice and beans)
USA: Fried Chicken and Cheeseburgers, peanut butter

South America

Argentina: Asado con Cuero (barbecued beef)
Bolivia: Humitas (corn pies)
Brazil: Feijoada (rice, black beans, meat and manioc)
Chile: Empanada (beef turnover)

Colombia: Ajiaco (vegetable soup)
Paraguay: Puchero (beef and vegetable stew)
Venezuela: Hallaca (cornmeal and meat cooked in banana leaves)

Africa

Egypt: Felafel (ground chickpeas and beans)
Ethiopia: Wat (spicy meat and vegetable stew)
Morocco: Bastila (pigeon pie)
Northern Africa: Couscous (steamed semolina) and Brik (fried meat turnover cooked with egg)

Southern Africa: Bredi (lamb and pumpkin stew) and Mealies (corn porridge)
Sudan: Ful (oil-cooked beans)
Western Africa: Fufu (ground cassava in sauce) and Peanut Soup

Europe

Austria: Schnitzel (breaded veal cutlet)
England: Yorkshire Pudding (meat drippings)
France: Bouillabaise (fish-based soup)
Germany: Sauerbraten (marinated pot roast)
Greece: Moussaka (eggplant, lamb and custard)

Italy: Pasta (noodles)
Poland: Pierogi (filled dumpling)
Romania: Mamaliga (corn bread or mush)
Scotland: Haggis (boiled lamb pudding)
Spain: Paella (chicken, fish and rice)
Sweden: Smorgasbord (cold buffet)

Asia

China: Won Ton (stuffed dumpling)
India: Curries (seasoned dishes)
Indonesia: Nasi Goreng (rice and side dishes)
Japan: Sashimi (raw fish)
Korea: Kimchi (fermented cabbage and fish)
Malaysia: Rendang (coconut milk beef stew)

Middle East: Kibbeh (ground wheat and lamb) and Shish Kebab (skewered meat and vegetables)
Philippines: Adobo (chicken and pork in soy and vinegar sauce)
Turkey: Baklava (honey and nut pastry)

Australia and the Pacific

Australia: Pavlova (meringue with fruit and whipped cream) and Vegemite (yeast spread)
New Zealand: Toheroa (green clam soup)
Polynesia: Poi (ground taro root)

Antarctica

Not applicable

* See photo at the beginning of the column.

Principal Crops			Origins of Sports	
Wheat	Tobacco	Corn	**Baseball:** Northeast USA, 1840s	**Lacrosse:** Canada, date unknown
Oranges	Peanuts*	Oats	**Basketball:** Springfield, Massachusetts: 1891	**Football:** United States, late 1860s
Sugar Beets	Potatoes	Grapes	**Volleyball:** Holyoke, Massachusetts, 1895	**Ice Hockey:** Canada, 1850s
Soybeans	Apples			
Cotton	Peaches			

Principal Crops			Origins of Sports	
Coffee	Maize	Rice		
Bananas	Soybeans	Wheat		
Sugarcane	Cacao Beans*	Nuts		
Cassava	Oranges	Grapes		

Principal Crops			Origins of Sports	
Cassava	Cacao Beans	Yams	**Bowling:** Egypt, as early as 5200 B.C.	
Sugarcane	Cotton	Olives	**Boxing:** Egypt, 4000 B.C.	
Plantains	Dates*	Grapes		
Millet	Palm Oil	Rice		
Bananas	Oranges			

Principal Crops			Origins of Sports	
Wheat	Tomatoes	Oats	**Bobsledding:** Switzerland, 1889	**Tennis:** France, around 1100
Sugar Beets	Maize	Oranges	**Track and Field:** Greece, Ireland, before 1300 B.C.	**Golf:** Scotland, 1450s
Potatoes*	Apples	Rye	**Alpine Skiing:** Norway, 1843	**Cricket:** England, late 1300s
Barley	Cabbage	Flax		
Grapes	Olives			

Principal Crops			Origins of Sports	
Coconuts	Jute	Wheat	**Wrestling:** Iraq (Sumeria), 2600 B.C.	**Soccer:** China, around 200 B.C.
Sugarcane	Rubber	Tea*	**Swimming:** Japan, 1600s	
Rice	Millet	Cotton	**Polo:** Iran (Persia), as early as 2000 B.C.	
Palm Oil	Spices	Onions		
Sweet Potatoes	Maize			

Principal Crops			Origins of Sports	
Wheat	Oats		**Australian Rules Football:** Ballarat, Australia, 1853	
Sugarcane	Apples			
Barley	Oranges			
Kiwifruit*				

Principal Crops	Origins of Sports
None	None

MAP INDEX (Selected Names)

Name	Index Reference	Page
Aconcagua (mountain)	B 3	56
Adriatic Sea	B 2	64
Afghanistan	C 3	69
Africa		61
Alaska	B 1	43
Algeria	B 1	61
Alps (mountains)	B 2	64
Amazon River	C 2	56
Andes Mountains	B 2	56
Angola	B 3	61
Antarctica		74
Arabian Sea	C 4	68
Aral Sea	C 2	68
Arctic Ocean		36
Argentina	B 4	57
Asia		69
Athens, Greece	C 3	65
Atlantic Ocean		36
Australia		73
Austria	B 2	65
Baffin Island	E 1	46
Baghdad, Iraq	B 3	69
Bahamas	B 1	53
Baltic Sea	B 2	64
Bangkok, Thailand	B 4	69
Baykal, Lake	E 2	68
Beijing, China	E 2	69
Belgium	B 2	65
Belize	B 1	51
Bering Sea	J 2	68
Berlin, Germany	B 2	65
Black Sea	C 2	64
Bolivia	B 2	57
Borneo (island)	E 5	68
Brazil	C 2	57
British Isles	A 2	64
Buenos Aires, Argentina	B 3	57
Bulgaria	C 2	65
Cairo, Egypt	C 1	61
Cambodia	E 4	69
Canada		47
Canary Islands	A 1	60
Cape Town, South Africa	B 4	61
Caribbean Sea	B 4	52
Caspian Sea	B 2	68
Central America		51
Chad	B 2	61
Chicago, U.S.A.	E 1	45
Chile	B 3	57
China	D 3	69
Colombia	B 1	57
Congo	B 3	61
Congo, Dem. Rep. of the	C 3	61
Coral Sea	C 3	72
Costa Rica	C 3	51
Cuba	A 2	53
Czech Republic	B 2	65
Danube River	B 2	64
Denmark	B 2	65
Dominican Republic	D 3	53
East China Sea	F 3	68
Easter Island	H 4	72
Ecuador	B 2	57
Edmonton, Canada	C 2	47
Egypt	C 1	61
El Salvador	B 2	51
Ethiopia	C 2	61
Europe		65
Everest, Mount	D 3	68
Fiji	E 3	72
Finland	C 1	65
France	B 2	65
Germany	B 2	65
Ghana	A 2	61
Gobi (desert)	E 2	68
Great Lakes	E 2	42
Greece	C 3	65
Greenland	H 1	43
Guadalajara, Mexico	B 2	49
Guatemala	B 2	51
Guinea	A 2	61
Guyana	C 1	57
Haiti	C 3	53
Hawaiian Islands	E 1	72
Honduras	C 2	51
Hong Kong	E 3	69
Honolulu, U.S.A.	C 3	45
Horn, Cape	B 4	56
Houston, U.S.A.	D 3	45
Hudson Bay	D 1	46
Hungary	B 2	65
Iceland	A 1	65
India	C 3	69
Indian Ocean		37
Indonesia	E 5	69
Iran	B 3	69
Iraq	B 3	69
Ireland	A 2	65
Israel	A 3	69
Istanbul, Turkey	C 3	65
Italy	B 2	65
Jamaica	B 3	53
Japan	F 3	69
Java (island)	E 5	68
Kalahari Desert	C 3	60
Kazakhstan	C 2	69
Kenya	C 2	61
Kilimanjaro, Mount	C 3	60
Kolkata (Calcutta), India	D 3	69
Laos	E 4	69
Liberia	A 2	61
Libya	B 1	61
Lima, Peru	B 2	57
London, England	A 2	65
Los Angeles, U.S.A.	B 2	45
Madagascar	D 4	61
Malaysia	E 4	69
Mali	A 2	61
Mauritania	A 2	61
Mediterranean Sea	B 3	64
Melbourne, Australia	D 4	73
Mexico		49
Mexico, Mexico	C 3	49
Mexico, Gulf of	E 3	42
Midway Islands	E 1	72
Mississippi River	D 2	44
Mongolia	D 2	69
Monterrey, Mexico	B 2	49
Morocco	A 1	61
Moscow, Russia	C 2	65
Mozambique	C 4	61
Mumbai (Bombay), India	C 4	69
Myanmar	D 3	69
Netherlands	B 2	65
Newfoundland (island)	F 2	46
New Guinea (island)	C 3	72
New Orleans, U.S.A.	E 3	45
New York, U.S.A.	F 1	45
New Zealand	E 3	73
Nicaragua	C 2	51
Niger	B 2	61
Nigeria	B 2	61
Nile River	C 1	60
North America		43
North Korea	F 3	69
North Sea	B 2	64
Norway	B 1	65
Oman	B 3	69
Ottawa, Canada	E 2	47
Pacific Ocean		72
Pakistan	C 3	69
Panama	D 3	51
Paraguay	C 3	57
Paris, France	B 2	65
Persian Gulf	B 3	68
Peru	B 2	57
Philadelphia, U.S.A.	F 2	45
Philippines	F 4	69
Poland	B 2	65
Portugal	A 2	65
Puerto Rico	D 3	53
Red Sea	C 1	60
Rio de Janiero, Brazil	C 3	57
Rocky Mountains	C 2	42
Romania	C 2	65
Rome, Italy	B 2	65
Russia	D 2	65
Sahara (desert)	B 1	60
Santiago, Chile	B 3	57
São Paulo, Brazil	C 3	57
Saudi Arabia	B 3	69
Senegal	A 2	61
Serbia	B 2	65
Seoul, South Korea	F 3	69
Shanghai, China	F 3	69
Siberia (region)	D 1	68
Singapore	E 5	69
Solomon Islands	C 3	72
Somalia	D 2	61
South Africa	C 4	61
South America		57
South Korea	F 3	69
Spain	A 3	65
Sri Lanka	D 4	69
Sudan	C 2	61
Suez Canal	C 1	61
Sumatra (island)	E 5	68
Suriname	C 1	57
Sweden	B 1	65
Switzerland	B 2	65
Sydney, Australia	D 3	73
Syria	A 3	69
Tahiti (island)	F 3	72
Taiwan (island)	F 3	68
Tanzania	C 3	61
Tasmania (island)	C 5	72
Tehran, Iran	B 3	69
Thailand	D 4	69
Tibet (region)	D 3	68
Tokyo, Japan	G 3	69
Toronto, Canada	E 2	47
Turkey	A 3	69
Uganda	C 2	61
United Kingdom	A 2	65
United States		45
Uruguay	C 3	57
Vancouver, Canada	B 2	47
Venezuela	B 1	57
Victoria, Lake	C 3	60
Vietnam	E 4	69
Volga River	C 2	64
Warsaw, Poland	C 2	65
Washington, D.C., U.S.A.	F 2	45
Wellington, New Zealand	E 4	73
West Indies (islands)	B 3	52
Yemen	B 4	69
Yukon River	B 1	42
Zanzibar (island)	D 3	60
Zambia	C 3	61
Zimbabwe	C 3	61